THE AMAZING WORLD OF
MONSTERS

FIONA
MACDONALD

CONSULTANT:
DR KARL SHUKER

LORENZ BOOKS

This edition is published by Lorenz Books

Lorenz Books is an imprint of Anness Publishing Ltd
Hermes House, 88–89 Blackfriars Road, London SE1 8HA
tel. 020 7401 2077; fax 020 7633 9499
www.lorenzbooks.com; info@anness.com

© Anness Publishing Ltd 2001, 2003

This edition distributed in the UK by The Manning
Partnership Ltd, 6 The Old Dairy, Melcombe Road, Bath
BA2 3LR; tel. 01225 478 444; fax 01225 478 440;
sales@manning-partnership.co.uk

This edition distributed in the USA and Canada by
National Book Network, 4501 Forbes Boulevard, Suite
200, Lanham, MD 20706; tel. 301 459 3366;
fax 301 429 5746; www.nbnbooks.com

This edition distributed in Australia by Pan Macmillan
Australia, Level 18, St Martins Tower, 31 Market St,
Sydney, NSW 2000; tel. 1300 135 113; fax 1300 135 103;
customer.service@macmillan.com.au

Publisher: Joanna Lorenz
Managing Editor: Gilly Cameron Cooper
Senior Editor: Nicole Pearson
Editorial Reader: Richard McGinlay
Series Design: John Jamieson
Designer: Margaret Sadler
Illustration: Stuart Carter, Chris Fossey, Peter Bull
Picture Research: Su Alexander
Photography: John Freeman
Stylist: Konika Shankar

Anness Publishing would like to thank the following
children, and their parents, for modelling for this book:
Troy Allick, Stacie Damps, Kiva Hussain, Mathew
Runyard, Jasmine Sharland.

PICTURE CREDITS
AKG, London: 5bl, 9tr, 42b, 49tl & 49br, 54bl, 55tl, 56bl;
American Museum of Natural History: 30t; Ancient Art &
Architecture Collection: 2t, 3b, 4r, 6, 9tl & 9bl, 12br,
13br, 14bl, 15c, 16, 30br, 38b, 39r, 42c, 43tr, 46bl & 49tr;
British Museum: 29b; George Brooker: 59bl; Christies
Images: 35bl; Corbis: 8l, 12bl, 13bl, 43tl, 52c; The Art
Archive: 43br; Mary Evans Picture Library: 5br, 8r, 19bl,
22b, 23t &23b, 35br, 39l, 43bl, 44b, 45tr, 48bl; Fortean
Picture Library: 14br, 23c, 26, 29tl, 35tr, 44t, 53bl; Ronald
Grant Archive: 18bl; Images Colour Library: 1, 2b, 3tl,
3tr, 4l, 5tl, 13tl, 14t, 15t, 18br, 28bl, 29tr, 31r, 32b, 34br,
34bl, 35tl, 44c, 45tl & 45b, 50bl, 55br; The Kobal
Collection: 31l, 40bl, 54br, 55tr; NHPA: 5tr, 28t; Oxford
Scientific Films: 52l, 53t & 53br; Ann & Bury Peerless:
15b; Rex Features: 58, 59tl & 59br; Victoria & Albert
Museum: 19tr, 49bl; Werner Forman: 9br, 12t,19tl.

AKG London: front cover main picture

Previously published as Discovery: Monsters

10 9 8 7 6 5 4 3 2 1

CONTENTS

What are Monsters?

If you hear giant footsteps, creaking doors, ghostly singing, or scaly wings flapping – look out, there may be monsters about!

From ancient times, people have imagined monsters in all sorts of shapes and sizes. Some monsters may be horrible just to look at, while others are dangerous as well. Many are macabre mixtures of different animals with magical powers, while others look like humans with enlarged, shrunken or distorted features. Many monsters are inspired by our worst fears and nightmares, such as wild beasts, dark forests, raging storms and unknown lands.

In the world of mysterious creatures, however, not everything is as it seems. Monsters may be as evil as they are ugly, but some strange beings are solitary and peaceful, and have a bad reputation only because they are different. The most hideous-looking fiend can turn out to be a true friend, whereas the most beautiful and captivating face can mask sinister intentions.

▲ THE MUMMY AWAKES

The story of an Egyptian mummy that comes back to life is told in the 1930s film *The Mummy*. Fantasy horror films and horror stories were especially popular during the 1930s, a time of economic crisis and social unrest.

◀ A MONSTER MISTAKE

A sea monster attacks a passing ship in this painting from the 1800s. In 1913, a real-life giant squid mistook the shiny grey hull of a ship for a whale. The suckers on its long tentacles (arms) could not grip the metal hull, and the squid accidentally swam against the ship's propeller and was killed. After this extraordinary incident, scientists began to investigate giant squid. They discovered that the creatures are extremely strong and can be very aggressive. They use their huge, beak-like mouth and five pairs of tentacles to catch their prey of whales and other sea creatures. Fortunately for sailors, giant squid rarely come to the surface. They usually live in the deepest, coldest parts of the sea, and cannot breathe properly or survive for long in warm or shallow waters.

SUPERNATURAL POWERS ▶

In many religious faiths, people believe that natural forces are the work of 'nature-spirits' with special powers. The frog-like kami is a Japanese nature-spirit that controls the winds and thunder. This kami, carved from ivory, is busy raising a storm. According to Shinto, the ancient religious faith of Japan, all natural forces – from small raindrops to mighty mountains – are controlled by kami. These supernatural beings can be gentle, kindly friends or strong, evil monsters.

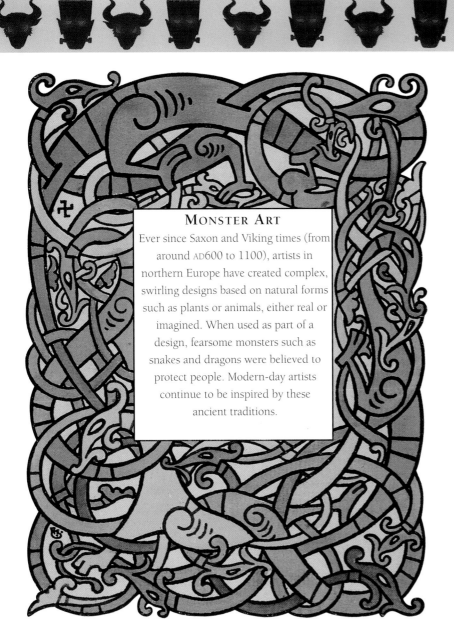

MONSTER ART
Ever since Saxon and Viking times (from around AD600 to 1100), artists in northern Europe have created complex, swirling designs based on natural forms such as plants or animals, either real or imagined. When used as part of a design, fearsome monsters such as snakes and dragons were believed to protect people. Modern-day artists continue to be inspired by these ancient traditions.

▲ REAL-LIFE MONSTER
The Orá, or Komodo dragon, is the largest living species of lizard in the world. Some people believe that it may have inspired many myths and legends about dragons. When fully grown, the male Komodo dragon reaches up to 3m in length and can weigh as much as 90kg. It lives only in dense rainforest on the Lesser Sunda islands in Indonesia. It is a meat-eater, and survives by catching other wild animals – mostly deer – with its sharp curved teeth. It can run fast, and smells disgusting!

◀ HUMAN MONSTER
People who are very powerful and who use their power in evil ways are sometimes called monsters. Adolf Hitler (1889–1945), the German leader during World War II, was often described as a monster by his enemies. Hitler's invasion of neighbouring countries led to the outbreak of World War II in 1939. He also masterminded the holocaust – an evil scheme to kill millions of minority peoples from German-ruled lands, including Jews, people with disabilities and gay people. Hitler killed himself in 1945, when he realized that Germany had lost the war.

▲ IN THE HALL OF THE MOUNTAIN KING
A fearsome troll king sits on his throne, surrounded by lesser trolls, elves and goblins. Trolls feature in many stories from northern Europe. They are people-eating monsters who live in mountain caves or lurk under bridges to snatch unwary travellers. In *Peer Gynt,* a story written in 1867 by Norwegian Henrik Ibsen, a young man called Peer leaves home to find adventure. He enters the trolls' kingdom, and meets the troll king, Great Boyg, who wants to eat him.

Monsters Everywhere

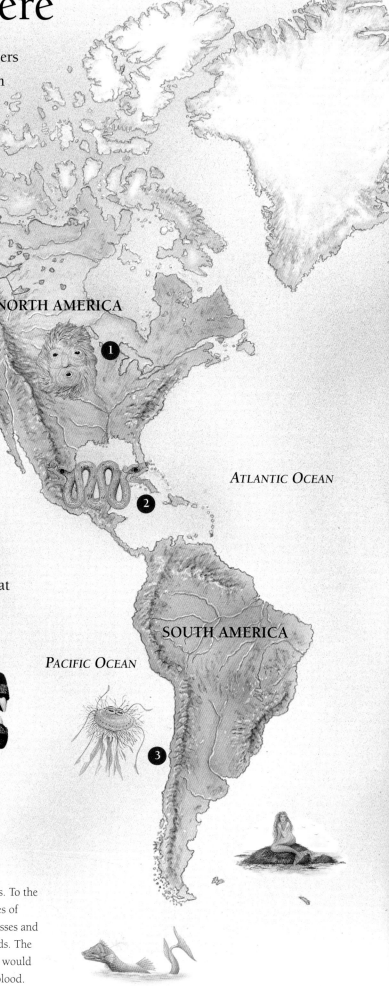

Poems, songs, pictures and carvings portraying monsters are found all around the world. Some monsters (such as dragons) look similar, but turn up in different forms in different countries. Others exist only in certain places. Dangerous monsters, weather-monsters and monsters that have a human-like form (such as giants) are widespread.

Look-alike monsters from different lands often have similar roles to play. For example, many butterfly-monsters symbolize the human soul. Sometimes monsters that look similar can have quite different associations in different lands. In Europe and the Americas, bat-monsters are linked with fear and death. However, in China, bats are not seen as monsters at all, but are believed to bring health, wealth and long life.

Wherever they are found, all monsters have a meaning. Sometimes this is religious. For example, in early Christian stories, goat-monsters represented wickedness, while in ancient Sumer (modern Iraq) people believed that the goat-fish monster Capricorn was their creator-god.

▲ SYMBOL OF LIFE AND POWER

In many parts of the world, people believe that snakes have monstrous qualities. To the Aztecs of Mexico, two-headed snakes represented lightning and rivers, examples of energy and power that came from the gods. Aztec warriors wore snake headdresses and pictures of serpents decorated temples where captives were sacrificed to the gods. The Aztecs performed sacrifices to please their gods and to ensure that life on Earth would continue. They believed that the gods sent energy for life in return for human blood.

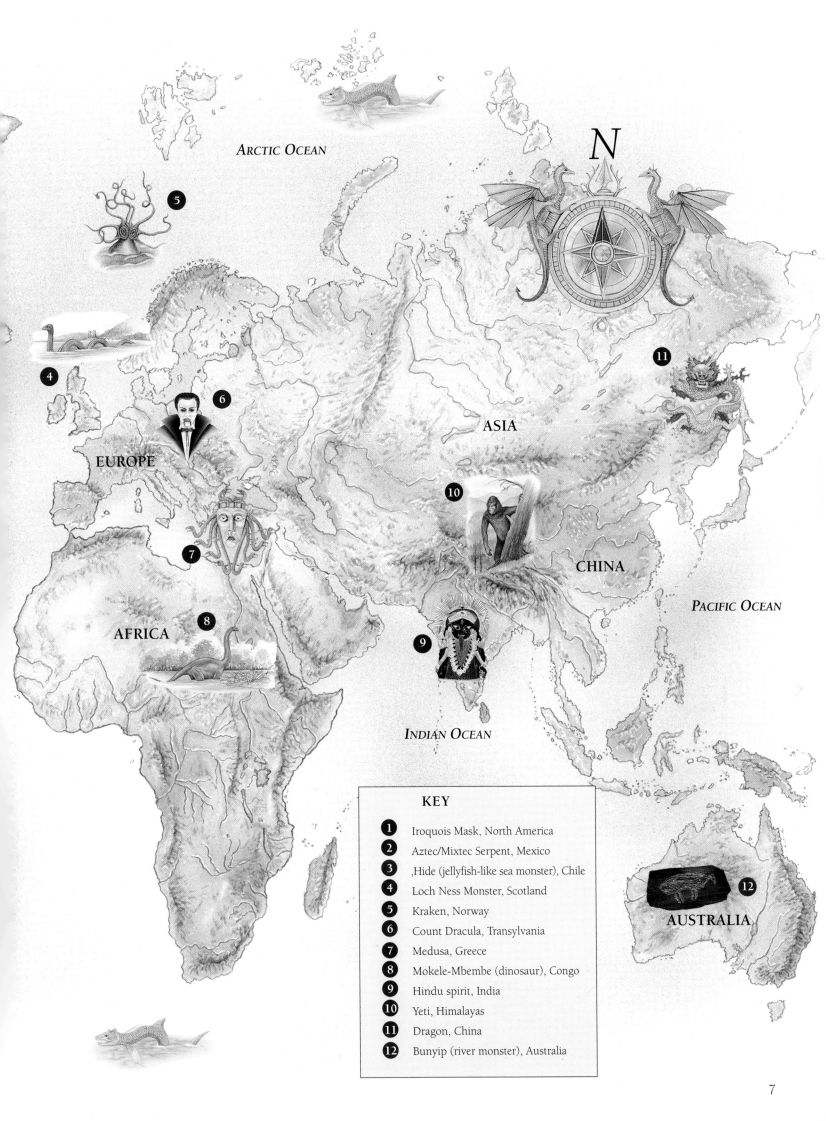

ARCTIC OCEAN

EUROPE

ASIA

AFRICA

CHINA

PACIFIC OCEAN

INDIAN OCEAN

AUSTRALIA

KEY

1. Iroquois Mask, North America
2. Aztec/Mixtec Serpent, Mexico
3. ,Hide (jellyfish-like sea monster), Chile
4. Loch Ness Monster, Scotland
5. Kraken, Norway
6. Count Dracula, Transylvania
7. Medusa, Greece
8. Mokele-Mbembe (dinosaur), Congo
9. Hindu spirit, India
10. Yeti, Himalayas
11. Dragon, China
12. Bunyip (river monster), Australia

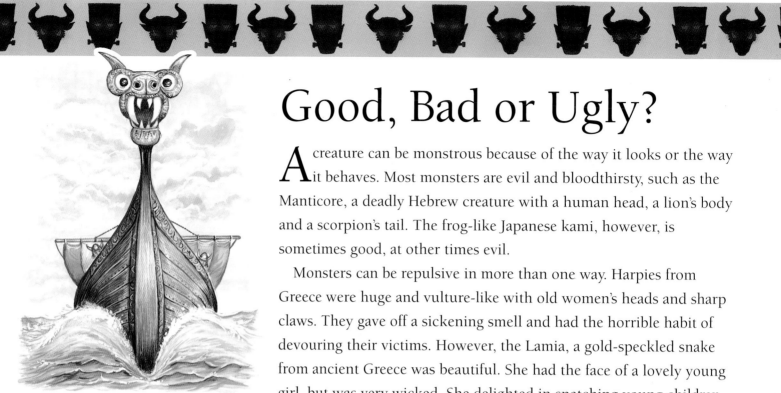

Good, Bad or Ugly?

A creature can be monstrous because of the way it looks or the way it behaves. Most monsters are evil and bloodthirsty, such as the Manticore, a deadly Hebrew creature with a human head, a lion's body and a scorpion's tail. The frog-like Japanese kami, however, is sometimes good, at other times evil.

Monsters can be repulsive in more than one way. Harpies from Greece were huge and vulture-like with old women's heads and sharp claws. They gave off a sickening smell and had the horrible habit of devouring their victims. However, the Lamia, a gold-speckled snake from ancient Greece was beautiful. She had the face of a lovely young girl, but was very wicked. She delighted in snatching young children from their mothers, and eating them.

Fierce monsters may be helpful to some humans, protecting their homes and families against enemies. Messenger monsters help living men and women to make contact with the spirits of the dead. Some creatures, such as the kind-hearted Beast in the fairytale *Beauty and the Beast*, may only be monsters because of some wicked sorcery.

▲ **SNARLING BEAST**
Fierce monsters carved on the prows of Viking warships strike fear into the enemy. Ship-monsters often resembled lions or dragons. They all had gaping mouths with long fangs and bared teeth. These terrifying monsters were probably meant to scare away evil sea-spirits as well as the people the Vikings attacked.

▲ **OFFERING TO A MONSTER**
In ancient China, Taotie were monsters with fearsome claws and horns. Taotie probably originated as the faces of people's ancestors pictured on cups used in worship ceremonies. Over the centuries the faces were transformed into monsters, possibly because people believed that their ancestor-spirits turned into monsters.

▲ **BEAUTIFUL BUT DEADLY**
Medusa was a type of female monster called a Gorgon. She was beautiful but had snakes instead of hair. Anyone who looked at Medusa was instantly turned to stone. She was killed by the Greek hero Perseus, who cut off her head. According to ancient Greek legends, the blood from Medusa's right-hand side was a powerful healing medicine, but blood from her left-hand side was a poison. Where it dripped on the ground, it gave birth to poisonous snakes.

SERPENT POWER ▶

A snake-monster with gaping jaws and giant fangs crawls along the front face of an Aztec temple in Mexico. For the ancient Aztecs, snakes were symbols of magical, life-giving power.

The Aztecs thought that a snake's ability to 're-create' itself by shedding its old skin as it grows larger and to appear fresh and young in a new one was magical. The Aztecs decorated many important buildings in Mexico with sculptures, carvings and paintings of writhing snakes.

◀ HAPPY HOME

Although this monster looks fierce, it is actually intended to be a symbol of wisdom, gentleness and happiness. Its name is Chi Lin, and it was made for a royal palace in Beijing, China, during the Ming era (AD1368-1644). Its horns are not dangerous. They represent the power of intelligence and bright thoughts shooting through the skull. This bronze model of a Chi Lin has four horns (the upper pair are double-pronged). Other Chi Lin statues have two or five horns. Many different kinds of monsters were used to decorate Chinese royal palaces. Most were placed on the roof, to scare away any evil spirits that might be trying to enter.

▲ GREAT APE

King Kong towers over a tall city skyscraper cradling a terrified woman in his hand. This ape monster first appeared in a 1933 movie. It told the story of a team of actors and film-makers who visit a remote tropical island. There they meet some giant, ape-like monsters called the Kong, and their leader, King Kong. Although he looked fierce and ugly, this enormous ape was really kind, gentle and romantic. He helped the film crew survive and even fell in love with the leading actress.

TOWERING TOTEM ▶

North-western Native Americans carve totem poles and place them outside the homes of high-ranking families. Totems are spirit-helpers and symbols of dead ancestors. They are often portrayed as monster animals and birds. Totem poles can be read like a book, retelling ancient stories about family origins. Living members of the family draw strength and pride from these stories, and from the totem-monsters who watch over their home.

Medusa Costume

In ancient Greek myths and legends, the Gorgons were three sisters, called Stheno, Euryale and Medusa. They were the daughters of two sea-monsters, and were beautiful, in spite of being monsters themselves. They had writhing, living snakes instead of hair, tusks like boars, gold wings and hands of bronze. Two of the Gorgons could not be killed, and lived for ever. But the youngest sister, Medusa, was killed by the Greek hero Perseus. He cut off her head, and gave it as a present to his guardian goddess, Athene. She wore it ever after like a monstrous brooch on the front of her cloak.

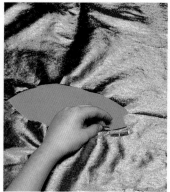

1 Fold the green fabric in half. Use a pair of compasses to measure out a semicircle with a radius of 4cm at the centre of fold. Cut out the semicircle.

2 Make small cuts along the edge of the hole, to create flaps. Fold each flap over and glue down. This gives the neck hole a neat, even edge.

You will need: 2 x 2m green fabric, pair of compasses, thick card, soft-leaded pencil, ruler, scissors, glue, dark green acrylic paint, pair of green tights, 40 pipe-cleaners, red card, needle and thread, green eyeshadow, lip brush, face paints in shades of green.

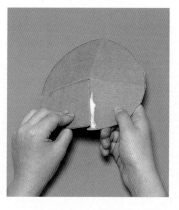

4 Set a pair of compasses at 7cm and draw a circle on to thick card (the side of a cardboard box will do). Then cut out the circle.

5 Cut into the centre of the circle. Bend the card slightly, overlap the two edges as shown and glue into position. Now paint the card dark green.

6 Cut the foot and about 20cm of the leg from a pair of green tights. Stretch it over the cardboard so the end of the foot is in the centre of the card.

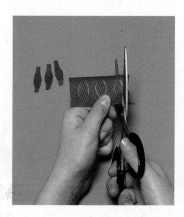

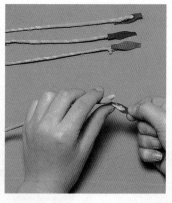

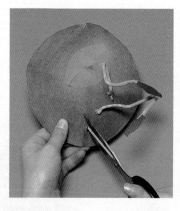

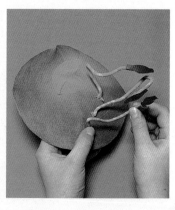

8 Draw small snake heads approximately 2.5cm long and 1cm wide on to red card and cut out. (You could fold the card over and cut out two at a time.)

9 Glue the red snake heads onto the ends of your pipe cleaners, as shown. Leave the 40 snakes for a while, until the glue has dried.

10 Use the end of a pair of scissors to make 20 small holes through the tights and card head piece. Take care to space the holes out evenly.

11 Poke a pipe cleaner through each hole. Bend the ends on the inside to hold in position. Form the pipe cleaners into twisted snake shapes.

3 Glue and fold over any fraying edges of fabric to complete the gown. Put the gown aside to dry while you make the head piece.

1 Paint green eye shadow over the eyelids, up to the eyebrows. Curl the outer edges upwards a little.

2 Using a thin lip brush, paint a darker green over your lips. Try increasing the size of your lips.

3 Paint snake shapes with a lighter green face paint. Then outline with a darker paint to finish.

7 Cut the remaining tights into strips. Wrap the strips around 40 pipe-cleaners as shown. Use a dab of glue on each end to secure the strips.

Now you are Medusa! You are so scary that anyone who looks at you will be literally frozen with fear. They will instantly stop in their tracks, with a look of pure horror on their face, as you turn them to stone. The only way that anyone can catch a glimpse of a Gorgon and survive is to look at their reflection in a shiny surface. Clever Perseus, who defeated Medusa, used his shield.

12 Curve the unused snakes into twisted shapes. Sew them all over the ends of the tights that hang around the card head piece, as shown.

Less than Human

Many monsters are part-human and part-animal. These weird mixed monsters often have the strength, agility or ferociousness of wild beasts. Several ancient monster-gods were pictured this way, such as the were-jaguars of the Olmec civilization in Central America. Some animal-human monsters were seen as 'totem spirits', who symbolized dead ancestors. They linked the grace, strength and sometimes magic qualities of certain animals to human families.

More often, mixed monsters are cruel. Their animal nature make them brutish (less than human). They lack the intelligence, kindness and honesty that the best humans possess. The ancient Greek Sphinx, for example, tested every person it met by asking them a riddle. Anyone who could not answer correctly was killed. Other stories about brutish monsters contained a moral message. In ancient Greek stories, the half-man, half-horse centaurs were savage creatures. This legend warned the Greeks of what might happen if humans let the wild, lawless side of their nature get out of control.

▲ **SNARLING, NOT CRYING**
The were-jaguar is part-jaguar, part-human baby. It was worshipped by the Olmec people, who were powerful in Central America between 1500BC and AD200. Other Olmec gods included a monkey-eating eagle and a dragon-like alligator. All the monster gods are portrayed with grimacing mouths and cleft (divided) heads.

HORSE OR MAN? ▶
To the ancient Greeks, centaurs were monstrous both in shape and character. They were aggressive, unintelligent creatures with the head and chest of a human and the body of a horse. Centaurs fed on raw flesh, fought each other all the time and flew into terrible fits of rage over tiny disagreements. The uncivilized centaurs, and their relatives, the shaggy, goat-like satyrs, were sworn enemies of the cultured Greeks. Centaurs feature in a number of modern stories too – they appear in both *Harry Potter and the Philosopher's Stone* and *The Lion, the Witch and the Wardrobe*.

▲ **DEMON IN DISGUISE**
The Hindu goddess Durga (the Impenetrable) tramples a defeated buffalo-monster underfoot with her eight arms raised triumphantly above her head. Durga was one form taken by Devi, the supreme Hindu goddess. The buffalo-monster is actually a wicked human-shaped spirit in disguise.

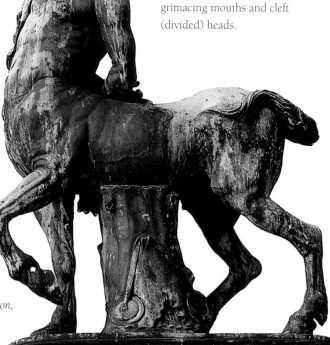

▲ MISMATCHED MONSTERS

The Sphinx (*left*) and Chimera (*right*) were each a very strange mixture of living creatures. Both of them appear in Greek and Roman myths. The Sphinx had the head and chest of a woman, the wings of a bird, and a lion's body. It perched on a gruesome nest of human bones while it lay in wait for travellers. The Chimera had the head of a lion, the body of a goat and a snake-headed tail. It killed anyone who approached it by breathing out fire. Today, the word chimera is used to mean a cross between two creatures, or a strange, fanciful idea.

▲ A FIVE-LEGGED FRIEND

A massive Lamassu (human-headed winged bull) guards the entrance to a royal temple in the ancient Assyrian city of Khorsabad (today called Dur Sharrukin, in Iraq). To the Assyrians, gateways were magical, dangerous places where good or evil forces might enter to threaten their king and his gods. So they built huge monsters like this to guard them. The horned cap on the winged bull's head is a sign of divine power, and its ability to scare away intruders. The artist who carved it has given it five legs so that, seen from the side, the creature looks as though it is walking. Seen from the front, it looks as though it is standing still.

DANCING ON DUTY ▶

Poised and ready for action, a half-human monster strikes a pose just like a boxer dancing into a ring. Monster figures such as this protected the tombs of important people during the Tang era in China (AD618–907). To Buddhist people of the time, they represented powerful spirits. Their task was to stop any evil forces disturbing the dead person's grave. This model is made of painted clay and stands about 1m high. It guarded the tomb of General Liu Tingxan, who died in AD728.

IS IT A BIRD...? ▶

A tunjo is half-bird, half-man. The Native American people of Colombia made small, golden statues of tunjos as offerings to their gods. Tunjos were buried with important people, and left in shrines and other holy places. All around the world, bird-shaped monsters linked people on Earth with gods who lived in the sky. They often acted as messengers for the gods.

Fabulous Animals

People have often believed that animals have special characteristics and, sometimes, special powers. Lions are seen as being strong and brave, beavers work very hard, horses are swift, intelligent and beautiful, and peacocks are imagined as being very proud.

Some animals were linked with particular gods and goddesses, and shared in their strengths, and a few animals were gods in their own right. Story-tellers made up tales about these animals, and artists and craftworkers created images of them to decorate precious objects such as totems, and important buildings and temples.

Few fabulous animals were like the real animals they were based on, although they sometimes had exaggerated natural features. The Hindu snake-creature Ananta, for example, had many heads instead of a real cobra's single one.

▲ HEARTY MEAL
The hungry monster Ammut (*right*) waits to gobble up a dead person's heart. In ancient Egyptian myths, Ammut sat beside the jackal-headed god Anubis, as he weighed dead peoples' hearts against a feather. Only the hearts that were light enough to match the weight of the feather balanced the scales. They belonged to truthful people who were then allowed to move into the next world. Owners of heavy, untruthful hearts did not. Their evil deeds meant that they did not deserve life after death.

◄ MANY-HEADED SNAKE
In Greek myths, the Hydra was a huge, poisonous, many-headed snake that terrorized the countryside and preyed on farmers' sheep and goats. The mighty Greek hero Heracles was sent by the king of Argos to kill this menace. First, he set fire to its lair by shooting burning arrows. This forced the Hydra out into the open. Then he started to cut off its heads with a sharp sickle. But for every head he cut off, two more grew in its place. So Heracles was forced to call on his nephew, Iolaus, to help him. Iolaus burned each neck-stump with a firebrand, so nothing would grow there, and at last the Hydra was destroyed. Ever afterwards, Heracles used the Hydra's blood as poison on the tips of his arrows.

▼ FIRE SERPENT
The Aztec fire-serpent Xiuhcoatl is coiled and ready to strike. This stone carving decorated a temple at Tenayca in Mexico around AD1450. The Aztecs honoured and feared many other nature-spirits. Snake-shaped Xiuhcoatl was believed to control thunder and lightning. In Mexico, as in many different lands, snakes were associated with rain and storms. Perhaps the zig-zag movements of snakes as they travel across the ground reminded early peoples of the jagged flashes of lightning in the sky and the flickering flames of a fire.

DOOM OF THE GODS

The monstrous Serpent of Midgard and the ravenous wolf Fenris face the Nordic gods Thor and Tyr, who are fighting to save the world. In Viking legends, the battle between the gods and a number of mighty monsters is the last struggle in the world's history. Thor and many other Viking gods fight bravely and eventually defeat the Midgard Serpent and Fenris. This terrible event is called the day of Ragnarok, which means 'the end of the world'. Afterwards, a giant wolf called Skoll swallows the Sun, the Earth is plunged into terrible darkness and desolation, and finally the world is destroyed by fire.

BEAUTIFUL BEAST ▶

Of all the fabulous creatures, the unicorn was one of the most beautiful. It was pure white, with a silky mane and gentle eyes. The unicorn looked rather like a horse, but it had a goat's beard, antelope hoofs, and a lion's tail. It was also brave, noble, loyal and wise. The unicorn's name means single horn, and this is usually shown growing in a twisted spiral from the centre of its forehead. Early Christian teachers in the Middle East claimed that unicorns could purify poisoned water by stirring it with their horns. Unicorn stories are reported from many countries and centuries. The most famous ones come from Europe during the Middle Ages (around AD1000–1500). According to these stories, unicorns could only be tamed by young girls.

◀ SAVED FROM A SERPENT

The Hindu god Vishnu leans on a multi-headed serpent-monster that he once overpowered. Vishnu is one of the three most important gods in Hindu religion. He preserves and protects the Universe, and is the god of love. According to Hindu myths, the newly created Earth (which took the form of a beautiful woman) was snatched by the serpent-monster. The creature dragged Earth down deep under the sea. She was saved by Vishnu, who took the shape of a giant boar. Vishnu crushed the serpent under his feet. Then he lifted Earth gently out of the water on his tusks, and carried her up towards the sky to greet the other gods.

Cat-bird Wall-hanging

The Paracas people, who lived in Peru from 400BC to AD200, decorated their clothes with strange cat-bird monsters, sea-creatures and snakes. It is hard to know what these monster decorations meant because the Paracas people left no written records to explain them. But archaeologists think that the monster-decorated clothes were worn only for religious ceremonies, and by dead bodies. This suggests that the animal monsters were either gods, guardian spirits, or family 'badges', which would help someone's ghost to be recognized by other family members in the world of the dead.

You will need: *piece of plain white paper measuring 21 x 15cm, soft-leaded pencil, paints, paintbrush, piece of thick card, sticky tape, scissors, piece of tracing paper, piece of red felt measuring 21 x 15cm, differently coloured pieces of wool, PVA glue, some scraps of coloured felt, felt strip measuring 1 x 21cm.*

1 Take the piece of plain white paper and draw your cat-bird design on it. Use the design shown on this page as a guide, or make up your own.

2 Decide on the colours you want for your design. First, paint the background. Here it is red, but you can use any colour you like.

Two thousand years ago, Paracas weavers produced beautiful embroidered fabrics. The wool was dyed and embroidered in a wide range of colours to depict monsters and creatures. These included many examples of strange creatures made up from the body parts of two different animals. Some fabrics show humans wearing gold nose ornaments that look like cat whiskers.

7 Now take the strands of coloured wool (which should match the colours of your painting). Cut the wool into strips, each about 15cm long.

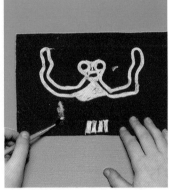

8 Using your original painting as a guide, cover an area of colour (for example, blue) with glue. Now gather together all the wool of that colour.

11 Glue the decorative pieces of felt into position as shown. They might represent the magic powers of your cat monster, or its strength.

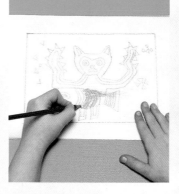

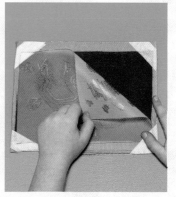

3 Use colours for the cat monster that will stand out from the background. Keep each area as a solid colour and allow the paint to dry.

4 Next tape the painting on to thick card to give it a solid base. Tape a piece of tracing paper over the top and trace your design in pencil.

5 Turn the tracing over and scribble all over the back with pencil. (Don't worry – you will understand why this is necessary in the next step!)

6 Tape red felt on to the card. Tape the tracing over the top, with the picture facing up. Draw over the lines of the picture again to print it on to the red felt.

The Paracas people used elaborately patterned fabrics for many other purposes, including clothing, wraps, bags, seats and bedding.

9 Place 4 or 5 strands together over the area of glue. If necessary, trim the strands to fit neatly into the intended shape. Do this for each area of colour.

10 Next, cut out some shapes from coloured felt. You could make little squares, triangles or circles, or cut out irregular shapes.

12 Cut out lots of 3cm-long strips of coloured wool. Take the 1 x 21cm felt strip. Glue the ends of the short strips of wool to the long felt strip.

13 Finally, line the back of the long felt strip with PVA glue and stick it on to the bottom edge of the tapestry. This is the tapestry's fringe.

Shape Changers

In the world of magic, monsters and make-believe, things are not always what they seem. Humans change into animals and monsters disguise themselves as humans. The ability to change shape is a sign of superhuman power. For example, the Celtic goddess Epona sometimes appeared as a horse and the Greek god Zeus transformed himself into many forms, including a giant swan, a bull and a shower of gold. Many horror stories, old and new, feature beautiful men or women who turn out to be vampires, harpies or monsters in disguise.

Changing shape was always a risky process. Fairy stories tell of humans trapped in monster shape by wicked spells, and of the dangers and difficulties they face in returning to their proper human form. Evil-doers were sometimes turned into monsters as a punishment, with horrible results. The Greek hunter Actaeon once caught sight of the goddess Artemis bathing in a lake. Furious, she turned him into a deer, and he was torn to pieces by his own hounds. Many other shape-changing stories end in tears, suggesting that some unfortunate humans and animals can never change their innermost natures.

▲ HEART-BREAKING BEAUTY

A selkie emerges from the sea to tempt a passer-by. In Scottish folklore, selkies were seals who transformed themselves into young girls and came ashore. They were so beautiful that men always fell in love with them, and sometimes married them, believing them to be real women. But selkies could not resist the call of the sea, however hard they tried. Eventually, they would slip away to rejoin their fellow seals, leaving their husbands heart-broken.

▲ SERPENT WOMAN

In this scene from *The Lair of the White Worm*, a serpent woman recoils from a crucifix. *The Lair of the White Worm* was written by Bram Stoker (1847–1912). It is the story of a white serpent who changes into a woman's shape at will.

BIRD OF ILL-OMEN ▶

Disguised as a menacing crow, the Celtic battle-goddess Morrigan croaks a harsh warning to the Irish hero Cúchulainn. Like many other gods and spirits, Morrigan changes her shape at will, and can become a black eel, a white heifer (a young cow), a grey wolf, a raven, an aged hag, as well as other creatures. As a bird, she was often seen flying above battlefields, looking for flesh to eat. In many countries, folk stories tell how crows and their close relatives, ravens, are unlucky and unclean, because they feed on the bodies of other dead animals. Their large size and powerful beaks make them look dangerous, and their loud, harsh cries can sound like human shrieks of pain. Crows often fly in large flocks, swooping fiercely across the sky, sometimes producing a terrifying effect.

▲ FEROCIOUS WILD BOAR

In Celtic Britain (around 800BC–AD100), wild boars were symbols of great strength and ferocious power. Celtic warriors sometimes fixed bronze boars to their helmets. By wearing these helmets, warriors believed that they would take on the boar's characteristics. The Celts also ate boar meat at religious ceremonies because they thought it would increase their strength and endurance. Some druids (Celtic priests) were known as boars, and Welsh legends tell of Twrch Trwyth, a wicked king who was turned into a boar as a punishment for all the cruel crimes he had committed.

▲ FOX-FAIRIES

A group of travellers falls under the spell of magical fox-fairies. Many stories from China and Japan tell of malicious fox-fairies who have the power to change their shape at will. Sometimes they appear as pretty young women and sometimes as gnarled old men. They are tricksters, luring humans to their doom. They pass straight through solid matter and can survive in air or water, as well as on Earth.

▲ WHO'S AFRAID OF THE BIG BAD WOLF?

The wolf disguises himself as an old woman, but will Red Riding Hood see through his evil plans? The story of Little Red Riding Hood was first written down around AD1690, but is probably much older. It describes the adventures of a girl who walks through a dark forest to reach her grandmother's cottage. She is warned to look out for wolves, but sees none. When she enters the cottage, she finds her grandmother strangely changed – into a wolf! The wolf has eaten her grandmother, put on the old woman's clothes, and climbed into her bed. Just as the wolf is about to eat Red Riding Hood, a woodcutter enters the house. He kills the wolf and releases the grandmother, unharmed, from the wolf's stomach.

▲ WOLF-MAN

In the dead of night, a ravenous werewolf hunts for living flesh to satisfy its hunger. Werewolves were men who lived a normal life for most of the time, but changed into wolves during a full moon. Anyone bitten by a werewolf would become one themselves. In Christian Europe, people believed that werewolves were possessed (controlled) by demons.

Shape-changing Puppet

Like many monster stories, the tale of Little Red Riding Hood deals with feelings we all can understand. Red Riding Hood has to walk through the dark wood, where unknown dangers lurk. Almost everyone knows the fear of visiting a strange place or being alone in the dark. At the end of her journey, we can imagine her horror when her loving grandmother seems to have changed into a monster!

In the early 1900s, glove puppets shaped like Red Riding Hood, Grandmother and the Wolf were popular children's toys. This clever puppet is actually two characters in one!

8cm — E   8cm — F
5cm   A   20cm
C   B
25cm   30cm   10cm
15cm   20cm   8cm   5cm   D

1 Copy these dress templates on to material using the measurements shown. Carefully cut out the pieces. Template A = fur body, template B = calico body, template C = patterned skirt, template D = patterned scarf, template E = wolf's arm, template F = grandmother's arm. Cut out two of each of templates A, B, E and F.

You will need: *grey fake fur, white calico, patterned material, scissors, air-drying clay, modelling tool (optional), polystyrene balls measuring 5cm in diameter, PVA glue, pencil, acrylic paints, paintbrush, white wool, 2 pieces of sponge 7cm x 13cm, 30cm-long balsa dowel (0.5cm diameter), string, 4 pipe-cleaners, thin card, needle and thread.*

6 Cut halfway through sponge widthways (keep two halves attached). Glue the dowel into the centre with 3cm sticking out at top. Glue sponge closed.

7 Repeat step 6 for the other end of dowel. Tie string around base of sponge and knot to make shoulder shapes of the puppet. Repeat for the other end.

8 Make holes with scissors through both sides of each sponge and thread pipe-cleaners through as arms. Bend and twist the ends to keep arms in position.

11 Cover the arms at one end of the puppet in the grey fur and the other in the white calico. Cover fraying edges with PVA glue to neaten them.

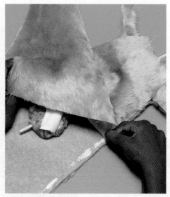

12 Slip the A templates over the end with fur arms and glue down the edges. Cut through the centre of one side so your hand can work puppet.

13 Glue along the edges of template B as shown. Slip over the other end of the puppet. Add calico arms to make the grandmother's top half.

14 Glue template C around grandmother's waist to make the skirt. Join the back of the skirt with back of template A (the side that you cut in step 12).

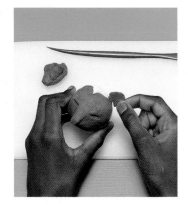

2 Press modelling clay on to a polystyrene ball. Mould the clay into the shape of a wolf's nose. Make holes for eyes and add extra clay for ears.

3 Let the clay dry. Then apply glue to the back of the head and cover it with grey fur as shown. Paint a wolf's face on the front of the head.

4 To make the grandmother's head, take the second polystyrene ball. Draw and then paint a simple face for the grandmother and allow to dry.

5 When the paint is completely dry, cover the top of the head with glue. Carefully stick white wool on the front section for hair, as shown.

9 Draw 4 pairs of hands for the grandmother and 4 pairs of wolf paws on to thin card and cut out. (Make sure to keep the hands in scale with the heads.)

10 Make large loose stitches along one long top edge of template C. Pull to gather up the fabric until the length is reduced to about 20cm.

Turn one puppet over to reveal the other. Your double-ended puppet can be used to dramatic effect when you perform the final scene of the Red Riding Hood story.

Make puppets of Red Riding Hood and the woodcutter in a similar way. You could make two separate puppets and then stage a puppet-show version of the Little Red Riding Hood story to entertain your friends.

15 Punch a hole in the head with the dowel, and glue both heads into position. Glue template D on to grandmother's head to make her head scarf.

Monstrous Places

The homes of most monsters are creepy and sinister, like the creatures that live in them. Entering these foul lairs can be highly dangerous. You might never escape.

In many legends, monsters live in wild, lonely places, far away from human villages or towns. The harsh, menacing landscape reflects the monster's character, and keeps intruders away. Some unusual monsters, such as trolls, live underground. Others hide in dense forests. Fantastic homes can even appear and disappear as the monster wishes, like the magnificent desert palaces conjured up by Arabian djinns (genies). Some homelands enchant visitors with their beauty in order to trap them there – like the magical land of Tir nan Og where Celtic 'little people' live. A few monsters' homes are monstrous themselves, such as the Sphinx's nest of human bones or Baya Yaga's house on legs.

The size of a monster's lair also reveals something about its owner. Massive giants live in towering castles, while tiny goblins shelter under low, grassy mounds. Vampires live in castles, too, where they soar and swoop around the walls as bats. They also spend nights haunting churchyards, hoping to find fresh blood.

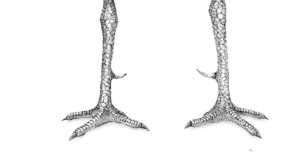

▲ HOUSE OF BONES

The terrifying house belonging to the Russian monster Baba Yaga is surrounded by a fence of human bones and perches on chicken legs so that it can walk and spin round. Baba Yaga is often portrayed as an old woman with a chicken's beak and chicken's claws for hands. Three horsemen also live in her sinister house. One is white – he is the Dawn – the second is red to represent the Sun, and the third is deep black for Night.

◄ DOWN A TROLL-HOLE

A foolhardy peasant boy stumbles upon a troll's home in a dark, dangerous network of tunnels and caves. The boy ignored his mother's warnings when he dared to explore a deep, underground hole. Like other monsters who live underground, trolls are large, strong, slow-moving and stupid, with huge appetites and bad manners. If they leave their homes and come to the surface, they feel confused in the fresh air and sunlight. Trolls are almost impossible to kill, however. This is because they can grow back arms and legs in a matter of days. During battle, any injuries they receive are usually healed magically before the fighting has ended.

◄ OUT OF THE CYCLOPS' CAVE

The Cyclops were one-eyed giants who lived in caves and made thunder and lightning. The Greek hero Odysseus was trapped by a Cyclops in his cave, along with the Cyclops' sheep. The Cyclops planned to eat him, but Odysseus escaped by a trick. He blinded the Cyclops, then hid in a dark corner. When the Cyclops let the sheep out to graze, Odysseus clung upside down underneath a ram's belly. Although the Cyclops checked each sheep as it walked out, he could not feel Odysseus through the ram's thick fleece.

BESIDE THE WATER OF DOOM ►

An old woman in black crouches by the side of a stream rubbing her hands together. Heaps of bloodstained clothes lie close by. She is the Washer at the Ford, who appears in many Celtic legends. Warriors who saw her as they marched off to battle knew they would not return alive because it was their blood she was washing away. Another Celtic monster, called the Banshee, also gave death-warnings. She was a female spirit whose weeping and wailing foretold death.

◄ SWAMP FIEND

The mighty, man-eating swamp-beast Grendel emerges from his bleak watery lair to snatch human victims. Grendel lived in a cave at the bottom of a lake. His killing sprees were eventually stopped by Beowulf, a brave Swedish warrior. First, Beowulf fought Grendel with his bare hands, tearing off an arm. Then he chased Grendel to his dank hiding place, where Beowulf was almost killed by the monster and his terrifying mother. Just in time Beowulf found a magical giant-made sword. He killed Grendel and beheaded his mother.

ON THE ROCKS ►

A beautiful girl sits on a rock beside a river combing her long golden hair and singing the sweetest, most haunting song. But things are not what they seem. The girl is a Lorelei, a beautiful but deadly creature described in German legends. According to these stories, the Loreleis' songs meant death. They lured men who heard them away from the river bank. The bewitched men jumped into boats and rowed towards the Lorelei, but were smashed to pieces on the rocks or drowned in the fast-flowing river.

Frankenstein's Laboratory

In his dark laboratory in an ancient German university, a wild-eyed student conducts terrible experiments, trying to bring dead human flesh back to life. As he connects an electric current to a patchwork body made of skin and bones stolen from graveyards, its eyes flicker and its limbs move. It is coming alive!

The student's name is Frankenstein, and from now on, he will never be free of the monster he has created. Although Frankenstein tries to escape from it, first to his home in Switzerland, and then to a cottage on a remote Scottish island, the Monster follows him. With its superhuman strength, it can roam anywhere in the world – even to the icy wilds of the Arctic. Appalled and despairing, Frankenstein finds he has no place to hide!

▲ **BODY SNATCHER**
Frankenstein returns to the university under cover of darkness. On night-time raids in churchyards, Frankenstein stole the healthiest body parts he could find, so that his monster would be strong.

◄ SUPERHUMAN

Frankenstein surveys his impressive monster, who is covered from head to toe in bandages. He made the creature much larger than life, measuring 2.5m tall, with a massive head and enormous hands and feet.

▲ EARLY ELECTRICITY

Frankenstein became fascinated by raging storms, and vowed to find out all he could about lightning and the electricity it contained. He observed many living things, such as huge trees, destroyed by the electrical power of lightning, and began to wonder whether electricity could also be used to bring dead things to life.

▲ SICKLY STUDIES

At university, Frankenstein worked frantically hard. He could not rest until he had used electricity to create life. He spent so long shut indoors with his books and his experiments that he grew pale, thin and sickly from lack of fresh air and exercise. His mind also became disturbed as he began to dig up rotting corpses and take them to pieces, to find out how human bodies worked.

Labyrinth Puzzle

The Minotaur was an ancient Greek monster with the body of a man but the head, horns and tail of a bull. He fed on human flesh. His mother was Pasiphae, wife of King Minos, who ruled the Greek island of Crete. When Minos discovered his wife's monstrous child, he hid it in a labyrinth, or maze. Once inside, the Minotaur could never escape.

Every year, young people from the Greek city of Athens were fed to the Minotaur. This hideous sacrifice was ended by Theseus, a brave Athenian warrior prince. You can imagine you are Theseus seeking the dreaded Minotaur in this puzzle game.

> **You will need:** piece of paper 35 x 50cm, pencil, ruler, piece of thin card 6 x 5cm, scissors, 2 pieces of thin card 9 x 3cm, felt-tipped pens in red, black and other colours, or paints, paintbrush (if using paints), 2 pieces of thin card measuring 3 x 1cm.

To defeat the Minotaur in his twisting, turning labyrinth, Theseus was helped by Ariadne, King Minos' beautiful daughter. Before Theseus set off into the labyrinth, Ariadne gave him a ball of thread. He tied one end to the entrance, and let it unroll behind him as he walked along. He reached the heart of the labyrinth, killed the Minotaur, and made his way back to the entrance, following the thread. He was the only person ever to get out of the labyrinth alive.

1 Fold the piece of paper in half lengthways as shown. Line up the edges carefully and run your finger along the fold so that it is a firm, sharp crease.

2 Unfold the piece of paper. Turn it around and fold it in half the other way as shown. Then unfold it again. Now you can see the centre of the paper.

7 Put the Minotaur head in the small square in the middle of the page. Draw around the bull's head in pencil. Now draw around Ariadne outside the large square.

8 Using a ruler, draw an indirect path leading to Ariadne from the opposite side of the board. You can make the path as complicated as you like.

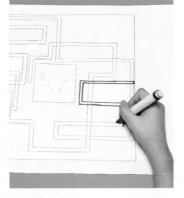

11 Fill in all the paths with a thick red felt-tipped pen, as shown. Or, if you have a steady hand, you could use red paint instead.

12 Paint the figures of Theseus, Ariadne and the Minotaur head with a single colour. Or you could use colourful felt-tipped pens.

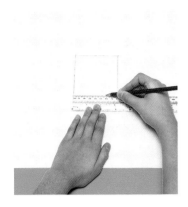

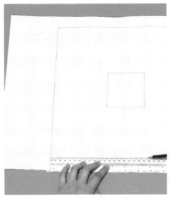

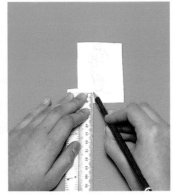

3 In the centre of the page, draw a square measuring 8 x 8cm, as shown. Make sure you keep the centre of the page in the middle of the square.

4 Draw a square measuring 30 x 30cm outside the first square. Again, make sure the centre of the page is in the middle of the square.

5 Take the rectangle of thin card measuring 6 x 5cm. Draw a Minotaur's head in the rectangle as shown. Then cut around the Minotaur's head.

6 Take the two rectangles of thin card measuring 9 x 3cm. Draw Theseus on one piece, leaving a 1cm square base, and cut out. Repeat for Ariadne.

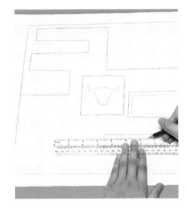

If you wish, you could add further decorative borders to finish as shown. Now set a challenge for your friends or family. Can they help Theseus find his way from one side of the board to Ariadne without meeting the Minotaur? You could time your friends to see who can do this the fastest.

9 Draw a second line along your path, about 1cm apart, as shown. Later on you will fill this in with pens or paints to make the path look solid.

10 Draw a second path leading from Ariadne to the Minotaur in the centre. Add further paths leading to dead ends or other parts of the board.

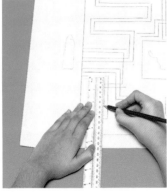

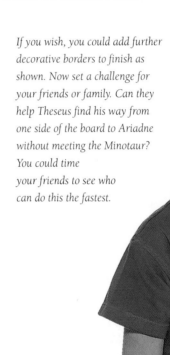

13 When the paint is dry, draw in the outlines with a black felt-tipped pen, as shown. Repeat for the Ariadne figure and Minotaur head on the board.

14 Take 2 pieces of thin card measuring 3 x 1cm. Make a cut at the centre of each and a cut in the base of the figures and slot together so they stand up.

Monsters of the Deep

The seas and oceans are some of the last unexplored regions on Earth. Almost three-quarters of our planet's surface is covered by water, and the inky black depths still contain many mysteries. Some genuine scientific discoveries seem almost too strange to be true – such as the small animals that live in the near-boiling water close to deep-sea volcanic vents. It is not surprising that generations of sailors have told fearful tales about sinister sights at sea.

Many sailors' stories originally had a basis in fact but grew wilder and more exaggerated each time they were retold. For example, legends about beautiful mermaids, with their women's bodies and fishy tails, were probably based on rare sightings of manatees (or sea cows), which live in warm waters. Manatees are large, slow-moving sea mammals with a gentle expression. Other seafarers' tales, such as those of people-eating whirlpools, warned sailors of real dangers at sea.

▲ NESSIE – FACT OR FICTION?

The Loch Ness Monster rears its head on its long neck. No one knows whether Nessie exists but many people claim to have seen it in Loch Ness, a deep lake in Scotland. There are even photos claiming to show the beast, but some of these are fakes. Several explorations of the loch have found no evidence that Nessie exists. Scientists say people might have mistaken an otter, a seal, a large fish, or a pattern of waves for Nessie.

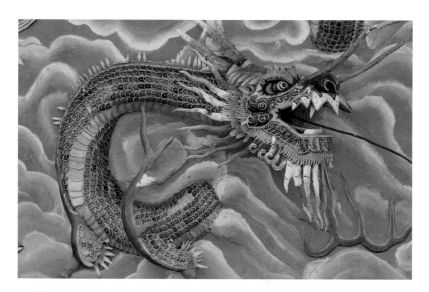

▲ WATER DRAGON

A writhing dragon leaps from the sea with a wild glint in its enormous eyes. In China and the Far East, dragons are seen as good monsters. They rule the seas and rivers, and they fly along rainbows, bringing thunder and making rain. Chinese stories tell how each dragon has a pearl – or raindrop – in its throat. Traditionally, Chinese people hold special ceremonies in springtime, on the second day of the second Chinese month, to ask dragons to send rain to help the crops to grow. They parade through the streets carrying rainbow-coloured paper dragons.

▲ THE KRAKEN WAKES

The giant kraken wraps its long, powerful tentacles around a ship to capsize (overturn) it. This terrifying monster was first described by Norwegian travellers around AD1100. They spoke of a lucky escape from a monster as big as an island. Others told how, from time to time, the kraken awoke from its sleep in the depths of the sea and surfaced close to an unlucky ship. It would then either eat the crew, or drown them.

▲ MYSTERIOUS MERMAIDS

A mermaid and a manatee meet under the waves. Mermaids appear in many stories. Some say their hair is green, while others report that it is blonde or golden brown. Some claim that mermaids are tiny – about the size of a four-year-old child, while others claim they are as tall as full-grown women. Many stories describe shy and gentle mermaids, but some claim that they are malicious and cunning, luring men into the sea to drown. Most stories agree, however, that mermaids are beautiful and rich. They live in underwater caves with precious stones and treasures they have taken from sunken ships.

▲ FROM THE OCEAN

An ancient map shows the dangers of the sea – and portrays enough sea-monsters to give even the toughest sailor a sleepless night. Of course, these monsters do not exist in real life. But it is easy to see how people might have imagined them. The ocean is full of extraordinary creatures, from enormous whales to bloodthirsty sharks and strangely shaped deep-sea fish. It is also a very threatening environment. Wild winds and waves can sink the strongest ships, and no one really knows for sure what lies hidden below the sea's surface. Sailors who returned from long sea voyages liked to entertain their friends with stories of amazing sights they had seen on their travels.

▼ MUSICAL MONSTER

A friendly-looking sea-monster with the body of a fish and the head of a dragon swims peacefully through the waves. This colourful object was made around AD1750 in Java, Indonesia, a country of islands and tropical seas. It is carved from wood and measures about 1m from nose to tail. Hidden inside is a gamelan, a set of 19 delicate gongs, played together to create haunting tunes. Gamelan music was used to accompany shadow-puppet plays, dance-dramas, feasts and special ceremonies at the Javanese royal court.

Fields and Forests

Long ago, fields were a place of life and death. People relied on crops growing there for survival. If a harvest failed, the whole community might starve. Many field monsters are therefore fertility figures. Plant monsters, such as European corn dollies or Native American corn-husk masks, are linked with rituals designed to protect the crops and encourage them to grow. They may be reminders of ancient fertility customs, in which chosen men or women were sacrificed to encourage the earth to produce plentiful crops.

Forests are places of mystery, magic and terror. They can be dark, vast, and unexplored. Trees can look monstrous, especially when they are gnarled and groaning in the wind. It is easy to understand how people came to believe that wild men, dinosaurs or other beasts might still survive in wooded areas. Forest monsters are usually shy, swift-footed and hard to see, such as the North American Bigfoot or Herne the Hunter, an early British monster that was shaped like a stag-headed man. Even today, horror films play on our fears of being left alone in a forest. In the *Blair Witch Project* (1999), for example, a group of students is terrified by a nameless monster among the trees.

▲ FOR CROPS AND CHILDREN

A powerful corn spirit peers out from a monster mask, made by Iroquois craftworkers in North America from dried corn (maize) husks. The mask was worn at mid-winter ceremonies, when the Iroquois lit fresh fires to mark the New Year, and held rituals. These were followed by masked dances performed by men belonging to the Husk Face secret society. As they danced, they asked corn spirits and spirits of the Earth to give them plentiful crops and many children.

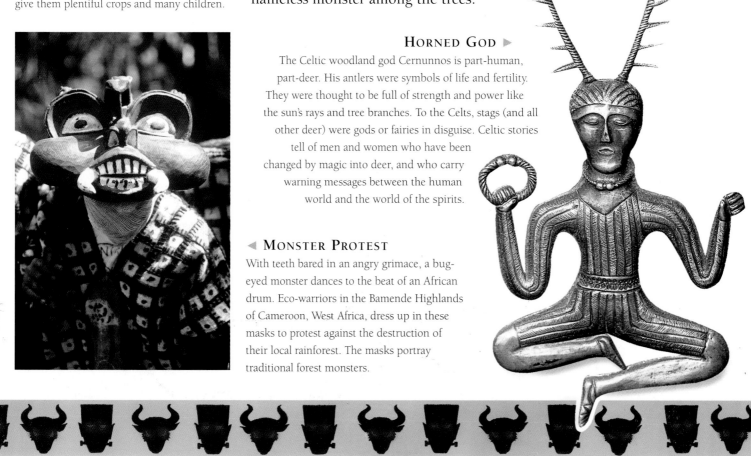

HORNED GOD ▶

The Celtic woodland god Cernunnos is part-human, part-deer. His antlers were symbols of life and fertility. They were thought to be full of strength and power like the sun's rays and tree branches. To the Celts, stags (and all other deer) were gods or fairies in disguise. Celtic stories tell of men and women who have been changed by magic into deer, and who carry warning messages between the human world and the world of the spirits.

◀ MONSTER PROTEST

With teeth bared in an angry grimace, a bug-eyed monster dances to the beat of an African drum. Eco-warriors in the Bamende Highlands of Cameroon, West Africa, dress up in these masks to protest against the destruction of their local rainforest. The masks portray traditional forest monsters.

◂ LIVING DINOSAUR?

For many years, people have claimed that a creature called the Mokele-Mbembe lives in the forests and swamps of the Congo in Central Africa. The environment here is similar to conditions on Earth 65 million years ago, when dinosaurs were alive. The Mokele-Mbembe is said to be about 9m long, with a long neck and small head. Traditional tales told by Congo hunters say that anyone who eats its flesh dies straight away. Several scientific expeditions have gone to the Congo to search for the Mokele-Mbembe. They have found some unusual footprints, but no clear evidence that this 'living dinosaur' survives.

◂ HAIRY GIANT

Bigfoot, or the Sasquatch, is a hairy giant reported to live in the forests of North America. Many people have claimed to see him, and even to have met whole families of huge, hairy beasts while hunting in the woods. Native American traditions also describe ape-like monsters. They are called the Taku He by the Sioux and the Wendigo by Native peoples in northern Canada. No Bigfoot bodies have ever been found, but in 1967, two men produced a film showing a tall, hairy creature, which they claim to have seen at Bluff Creek, California. Some scientists believe this film might be genuine evidence, while others suspect that it is a fake.

▲ WILD MAN OF THE WOODS

Who goes there? The old English Wodewose, or Woodiwiss, was one of many wild men who were rumoured to live in woods and forests throughout the world. They looked like humans, but were unable to speak any understandable language. Today, wild woods are rare in Europe, but until medieval times (from around AD1000 to 1500) forests covered large areas.

Green Man Plaque

The Green Man was an ancient forest spirit, guardian of trees and woods. He is seen in many forms, including carvings and paintings.

Originally, the Green Man may have been a Celtic god, or a spirit worshipped by peoples who lived in Europe before the Celts. As a guardian, he was kindly and protective. But he had another, more sinister, side. Like the rest of nature, he could be mysterious, unpredictable and cruel. The Green Man's severed head may have been a reminder of the grim Celtic custom of head-hunting, when warriors carried home the heads of their enemies after battle.

1 Draw a square measuring 20 x 20cm on to white paper. Draw the eyes, nose and mouth of the Green Man in the centre of the square, as shown.

2 Draw decorative leaf shapes all around the face. Then draw two leaves on stalks coming out of the mouth of the Green Man, as shown.

You will need: soft-leaded pencil, ruler, piece of white paper measuring approximately 23 x 23cm, sticky tape, thick card, tracing paper, air-drying clay, rolling pin, plastic or wooden chopping board, modelling tools, light grey or green and dark green paint, paint brushes, PVA glue (optional).

7 Use a modelling tool to cut into the clay around eyes, nose and mouth. Cut at different depths for various effects but do not cut right through the clay.

8 Roll out some more clay for the eyes. Stick them on with water. Roll out some thin, snake-like pieces of clay for eyebrows and stalks coming out of mouth.

9 Roll out some more clay to an even thickness of 0.5cm. Trace the leaf shapes from your design on to the clay, using the method described in Step 6.

The leaves sprouting from the Green Man's face were images of springtime and new life. They also showed how new life could spring from dead, decaying flesh. Models of the Green Man were carried in May Day festival processions in England, where they were also known as Jacks in the Green.

11 Stick the leaf shapes in position on the face plaque. Curve the leaves up at the edges to make them look realistic, as shown. Leave to dry.

12 Paint the clay plaque light grey or green and leave to dry. Then begin painting the face and background leaves a darker shade of green.

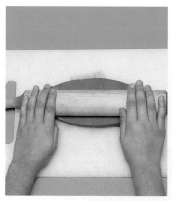

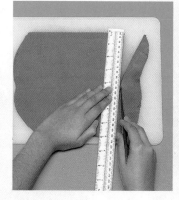

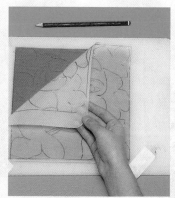

3 Tape your drawing on to card and tape tracing paper on top. Trace your design. Turn the tracing over and draw over the lines on the other side for later.

4 Roll out a piece of air-drying clay on a plastic or wooden chopping board. Roll the clay evenly until it is approximately 1cm thick all over.

5 Now take the ruler and a modelling tool with a blade-like point. Cut out a square measuring 20 x 20cm. This will be your plaque.

6 Position your tracing over the top and tape it down. Draw over the design and the lines should come through on to the clay underneath.

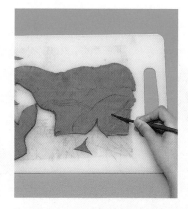

10 Put the clay on the chopping board so you do not cut into the table or work surface. Use a modelling tool to cut out leaf shapes.

Images of the Green Man sometimes appear in Christian churches. Although the Green Man is a pagan (pre-Christian) figure, he may be there as a reminder of the darker, wilder side of human nature that exists alongside peoples' wish to be good and truthful.

13 Outline the leaves with black paint to finish. You could also paint your plaque with PVA glue to give it a varnished (shiny) look.

Sky Monsters

Some of the fastest, strongest, most beautiful birds are killers. They swoop down suddenly from a vast height to snatch their unsuspecting prey from the ground and carry them away. Sky monsters such as the Arabian roc, the Greek harpy and the Persian Simurgh behaved just like this. They resembled birds of prey, but were much bigger. The fearsome cockatrice from ancient Rome was a snake with the head, wings and legs of a cockerel. It did not fly very far or fast, but it killed anything it met.

Other mighty, flying creatures were helpful and protective towards humans and gods. The Indian Garuda bird carried the fire-god Vishnu on its back, and fought against dangerous snake spirits. Griffins were fierce to look at, but they guarded human treasures. Chinese dragons brought wisdom and knowledge to humans, as well as rain. Many sky monsters, for example, the North American Thunderbird, were linked to the weather.

▲ SNATCHED FROM THE SEA

A roc snatches Sinbad the Sailor from a shipwreck and carries him to safety. Rocs (or rukhs) were believed to be enormous birds that were strong enough to carry three elephants at once. They are described in many stories from the Middle East, and in tales told by travellers who crossed the Indian Ocean. Rocs could be kindly or dangerous. Some sank ships by dropping huge boulders on them.

◀ GUARDIAN OF GOLD

Griffins were monstrous birds with the heads, wings and claws of an eagle, and the body of a lion. Like eagles, they were lords of the sky and were sacred to the Sun god. They were brave and watchful. Like all sky monsters, they had excellent eyesight. Griffins guarded the gold of India and the treasures of the Scythians, a nomad people who lived in Central Asia who were famous for their goldworking skills.

▲ HAPPY DRAGON

A huge dragon kite is carried in a spring festival procession in Singapore. In many Far Eastern countries, dragons are symbols of happiness, wisdom and fertility. They represent life-giving natural forces, especially rain. Dragon kites always have large, shining eyes. People believe they are keen-sighted and watchful. For this reason, dragons are good guardians.

HUNGRY HARPIES ▶

According to Greek and Roman legends, harpies were the two goddesses of wind and rain. Their names were Storm and Swift-Flying. They were sisters of Iris, the rainbow, who was often sent to Earth as a messenger by the gods. Iris was gentle and beautiful, but the harpies were ugly and cruel. They were sent to punish people who had angered the gods. They swooped down from the skies to snatch children, or any other food they could get their claws on. They were always hungry, as their appetites could never be satisfied. Wherever they went, the harpies left behind a horrible smell.

▲ IMMORTAL HORSE

The winged horse Pegasus was born from the blood of Medusa's head. At first, it was wild and dangerous, but the ancient Greek hero Bellerophon tamed it. They had many adventures together, until Bellerophon became too ambitious. He asked Pegasus to carry him to the top of Mount Olympus, where the gods lived. Zeus, the king of the gods, was angry. He sent a fly to sting Pegasus and drive the horse wild. Bellerophon fell off and died. From then on, Pegasus lived with the gods, and pulled Zeus' chariot across the sky.

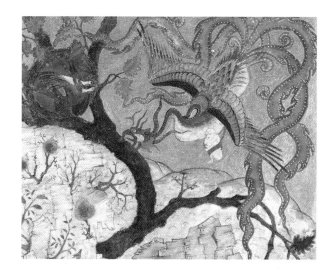

▲ QUEEN'S COMPANION

The Simurgh bird nested in the Tree of Knowledge. This bird had glittering feathers, a human face, two sets of wings, vulture claws and a peacock tail. It was supposed to live for ever and to see the world destroyed and reborn three times. The Simurgh often carried away children, but did not harm them. One particular Simurgh was the chosen companion of the extremely wealthy Queen of Sheba, a monarch mentioned in the Bible who may have reigned in Ethiopia.

DRAGON THIEF ▶

A flying dragon carries an empress high above the rooftops in a scene from a traditional tale from Serbia, Europe. All around the world, dragons are seen as lords of the sky. In Europe and China, they are usually portrayed with huge wings, which give them the power to fly in spite of their heavy, scaly bodies and long tails. Dragon wings are feathered like an eagle's or are made of leathery skin, like the wings of a bat. In Japan, dragons are wingless, but can still rise magically into the air.

Chinese Dragon Kite

In Chinese legends, dragons were the link between the sea and sky. In winter, they lived in rivers and streams. In springtime, they flew among the clouds, like kites. For centuries, Chinese people have made dragon kites like the one in this project.

Usually, dragons were kindly, but if humans annoyed them, they could make the clouds drop all the rain they carried, and cause terrible floods. They could also collect up all the world's water in magic baskets to cause droughts, and turn day into night by swallowing the sun. Dragons could become as large as the universe, or as small as a caterpillar.

1 Bend two pieces of bendable wire, each measuring 109cm, into a ring. Tape the ends together. Repeat with pieces measuring 92cm, 78cm and 64cm.

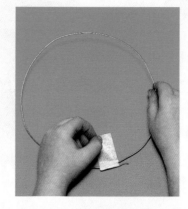

2 Glue together each pair of balsa wood rods to make a cross. Then tie each cross with string to secure. You should have 5 wooden crosses in all.

You will need: *a piece of bendable wire 452cm long, sticky tape, 0.5cm diameter balsa wood rods in the following sizes: 4 x 36.5cm; 2 x 30.5cm; 2 x 25.5cm; 2 x 21.5cm, string, scissors, PVA glue, soft-leaded pencil, coloured paper, white paper.*

6 Draw around one of the two largest rings on to white paper to create the template for the dragon's face. This will be the front of your kite.

7 Draw the outside of your dragon face within the circle. Try to make it as large as possible, to fill all the available space. Draw in the eyes next.

8 Draw in each section of the face as separate pieces – this is because you will need to cut them out later. Draw the nose and the lower part of the nose.

11 Put glue on the back of the yellow face and stick on to the front ring (this is one of the two larger rings). Make sure it is positioned in the centre.

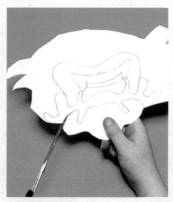

12 Now go back to your template again and cut out the nose, as shown. Then trace it on to red paper. Cut the nose out from the red paper.

13 Glue the red nose on to the centre of your dragon face, as shown. Continue cutting out the template pieces to make the rest of the face.

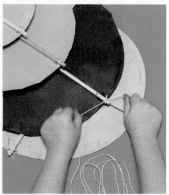

14 Stagger the rings on top of each other with the largest at the back and the end of each rod 10cm apart. Tie together and repeat for each rod in turn.

3 Pair up each cross with a wire ring of similar size. The ends should overlap by about 1.5cm. Glue and tie each ring to its wooden crosspiece.

4 Place a piece of coloured paper under each wire ring. Draw around each ring. Cut out the circle leaving a 2cm border all the way around.

5 Glue each wooden cross on to its paper circle. Snip along the edges of the circles. Fold them over the ring and glue them down to finish.

9 Draw in the lower part of the dragon's mouth and the teeth. You could make it kindly ... or scary! Do not forget to add horns on the side of the face.

10 Cut out the face and the eyes, as shown. Place it over some yellow paper and trace around the outside. Then cut out the face shape from the yellow paper.

To finish your dragon kite, tie the end of a ball of string to the tip of the bridle. This will be your flying line, which will allow the kite to soar high into the sky.

No one knows for sure but it is believed that kites were first invented in China. The earliest kites were made of woven silk or paper, made rigid by bamboo or reed sticks. Chinese kites were used in festivals, to send messages, and even to carry people, as spies in wartime.

15 Turn the kite over. Tie three 30cm lengths of string to the ends of three rods at the front. Tie them together at the end to make a bridle.

The ancient Chinese believed that dragons would drive away evil spirits. They were also a symbol of royal power. Only emperors and their close family were allowed to wear robes decorated with dragons.

Monster Meals

What do monsters eat? Some of the nastiest, fiercest monsters eat people! In particular, giants and ogres are supposed to enjoy the taste of human flesh. Many other monsters, from European dragons to deep-sea serpents, enjoy eating people for dinner, too. Cannibalism (the practice of humans eating other humans) is strictly forbidden in most cultures. Anyone who dares to do so becomes cursed and outcast. Often, they are called monsters, too.

As well as eating human flesh, many monsters drink blood. All around the world, blood is seen as sacred. It is a symbol of life, containing divine, life-giving energy. In many civilizations, people believe that blood contains a person's spirit. By drinking it, a monster is stealing away their life-force.

A few monsters use their supernatural strength to protect food and water supplies for fortunate human beings. Rare, mysterious monsters, such as the Middle Eastern phoenix, shun ordinary food but consume themselves so that they will live for ever. A snake monster called the Ouroboros is usually shown eating its own tail. This is a symbol of the creature's everlasting life.

▲ OUT FOR BLOOD

A giant looms over his tiny victim, shouting and stamping and swinging his heavy club. Giants appear in legends from many lands. Usually, they were fierce, brutal and clumsy. Often, they ate human flesh. In ancient British folk tales such as *Jack and the Beanstalk*, giants were too big and strong to fight against, but could be defeated by cleverness and quick wits. Their cries of 'Fee, fie, foe, fum! I smell the blood of an Englishman!' may be based on ancient Celtic magic spells.

▼ FOR HOLDING HEARTS

A half-human monster leans backwards with a horrid grin. This stone carving is an Aztec chac-mool and once, long ago, it would have received still-beating human hearts. Chac-mools stood close to temples in Aztec and Toltec lands (present-day Mexico). The Aztecs, like other central American peoples, believed that it was their duty to feed their gods with human hearts and blood. If they did not do this, they thought the world would come to an end. Chac-mools often had huge goggle-eyes, similar to those of Tlaloc, the Aztec god of rain.

▲ BLOOD-SUCKER

The vampire Count Dracula prepares to bite the neck of his latest victim. Vampires feature in many books and films. They are dead people who have come back to life and must suck the blood from living people to survive. Anyone bitten by a vampire becomes one, too. South America is home to a real-life blood-sucker – the vampire bat. It bites sleeping animals such as pigs or cows and laps up their blood with its tongue. When it bites, the bat can pass on deadly diseases, such as rabies.

FIERY FOOD ▶

The phoenix was a huge, male bird that lived for 500 years. When the time
came for it to die, it built a nest out of sweet-smelling twigs and herbs, set
fire to it, then climbed on top. As the old phoenix burned, its body and the
flames from the fire gave it food and energy to recreate itself. After three days
it was reborn and ready to live again. Jewish legends link the phoenix with
food in a different way. They say that it lived so long because it refused to eat
the forbidden fruit in the Garden of Eden. Legends about the phoenix may
have originated in the ancient Egyptian city of Heliopolis. That was a centre
of Sun worship, where animals were sacrificed by being killed then burned
in front of a holy altar. People believed that the smoke from the burning
sacrifice drifted up to the gods in the heavens.

◀ DOG EAT DOG

In Greek and Roman myths, a fierce, three-headed dog called Cerberus
guarded the entrance to Hades (Hell). Poison dripped from his fangs, his
tail was a hissing snake, and he had snakes, instead of a collar, wrapped
around his neck. In one famous Roman poem, Cerberus falls asleep after
eating a cake of honey and poppy, given to him by a a wise woman,
leaving Hell's gate unguarded. Cerberus was one of several horrid hell-
hounds. The ancient Greeks and Romans left offerings of food at
crossroads to make sure these hell-hounds did not attack dead souls.
The favourite offering was a dead dog.

◀ DRAGON'S DRINK

In China, one of the most famous types of tea is
called *Longjin* (Dragon's Well). It is produced
near the city of Huangzhou, in southern China.
In Chinese stories, dragons often acted as
guardians of wells or lakes where the waters were
especially pure, or were said to have magic
powers. Lakes and wells were also believed to be
magical, dangerous places. They were gateways
between everyday life and the magic world of
monsters and spirits.

Anti-vampire Food

In many countries, garlic is believed to have magic powers. It protects against snakes, lightning, the evil eye (a curse sent by looking), and vampires. In the past, people hung bunches of dried garlic as a lucky charm in their homes and carried a clove of garlic in their pocket, in case they met a vampire. Today, some doctors believe that raw garlic is good for our health – they say that it has germ-killing powers.

You can protect yourself from vampires, too, with these simple garlic recipes, and have a delicious meal. Ask an adult to help you with the cooking.

> *You will need:* pan, 30ml olive oil, 8–9 garlic cloves, wooden spoon, 4 small slices of bread (or 4 halves of bread roll), 15ml paprika, 600ml beef or vegetable stock, 5ml cumin, plastic or wooden chopping board, salt and pepper, 4 bowls and spoons, chopped fresh parsley or basil, small French loaf, bread knife, 50g butter or margarine, mixing bowl, knife for spreading, silver foil, baking tray or baking sheet.

1 Heat 30ml of olive oil in a pan. Add 4 whole cloves of garlic and fry until golden brown. Remove the garlic from the pan and set aside.

2 Fry 4 small pieces of bread or 4 halves of bread roll in the same oil until they have turned golden. Remove the bread from the pan and set aside.

7 Add the pieces of crushed garlic to the pan of beef or vegetable stock. Try not to get the garlic on your fingers, as it leaves a strong odour.

8 Season the mixture in the pan with salt and pepper. You will not need much salt (if any) because the stock will have salt in it. Cook for 5 minutes.

Bloodthirsty vampires appear in legends from many different lands. In Europe, Count Dracula lives in Transylvania (a region of Romania), preying on visitors to his castle. Indian stories tell of female vampires who weaken sleeping men by sucking blood from their toes. Other examples of the living dead occur in African and Caribbean stories. They describe zombies – corpses that have been brought back to life by magic. They walk with stiff, jerky movements and obey one person only – the magician who revived them.

12 Put down a chopping board and carefully peel 4–5 cloves of garlic. Crush the cloves under a wooden spoon to break them up, as shown.

13 Mix the crushed garlic in to 50g of softened butter or margarine. You could heat the butter in a pan to soften it, or microwave it for a few seconds.

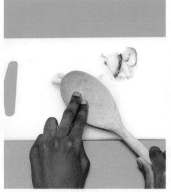

3 Fry 15ml of paprika in the same pan for a few seconds. Use a low heat and do not overcook or the flavour of the paprika will be lost.

4 Stir in 600ml of beef stock (make this using the instructions on the packet). If you do not eat beef, you can use vegetable stock.

5 Add 5ml of cumin. This spice will add a really special flavour to the soup. Put the pan aside and return to the cooked garlic cloves.

6 Place the cooked garlic cloves on a chopping board. Crush them under a wooden spoon to break them up into smaller pieces, as shown.

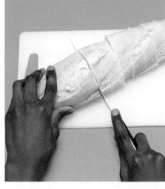

Some experts say that garlic is good for the heart and blood.

garlic cloves

garlic bulb

9 When the soup is cooked, ladle it into 4 bowls. Place a piece of the bread in the centre. This will soak up some of the soup and will be delicious.

10 As a final touch, garnish the soup in each bowl with a little chopped fresh parsley or basil leaves. Now your soup is ready to serve.

11 Slice a small french loaf all the way along. Make sure not to cut all the way through, so that the segments remain attached to each other.

Protect yourself from vampires by eating this delicious meal, because the only way to kill a vampire is by burning, exposing it to sunlight or stabbing it through the heart with a wooden stake!

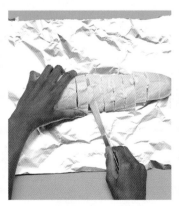

14 Place the half-sliced loaf on to a piece of foil large enough to cover it. Spread the garlic butter in-between the half-sliced segments.

15 Wrap in the foil. Put in a preheated oven at 190°C/ Gas 5 for about 10 minutes, or until all the butter has melted and the bread is a golden colour.

Monsters in Love

Monsters are fierce, ugly and come in all manner of shapes and sizes. Yet there are still many famous love stories concerning monsters. Usually, the monster is besotted by a human, but sometimes it is the other way round. Often monster love stories contain hidden messages. *Beauty and the Beast* shows that true love can make even the most unlikely person handsome. Tales such as the Scots *Tam Lin* praise courage in love. A few stories show how women can take great risks for the sake of love. For example, the Phoenician princess Europa deserted her family and friends for love, and ended up a proud mother, and a queen. Other stories tell of heroes who save maidens from savage monsters, and live happily ever after with them. Sometimes, the love between two humans gives them the power to defeat an evil force. In the fairy story *Hansel and Gretel*, the love between brother and sister helps them escape from a trap set by a monstrous witch.

▲ BONNY TAM LIN

The Scots ballad *Tam Lin* tells how Janet's boyfriend, Tam, is captured by the Queen of the Fairies. She is jealous of their love. Helpful magic creatures advise Janet how to get Tam back. She must seize him by moonlight, when he rides out with the Fairy Queen. Then she must hold on to him, whatever happens. This she does, even though the Fairy Queen turns Tam into water, then a blazing fire and finally a lion. In the end, the Fairy Queen admits defeat, and Tam becomes human again.

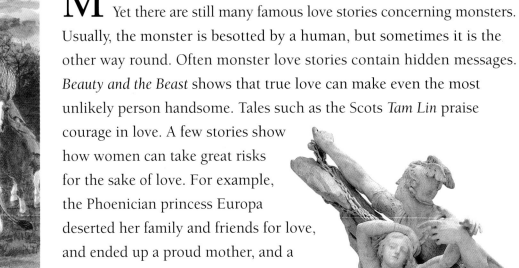

◀ BEAUTIFUL BULL

Phoenician Princess Europa rides across the waves on the back of a beautiful bull – actually the Greek god Zeus in disguise. Zeus had seen Europa walking on the seashore with her friends. He fell in love straight away. Transforming himself into a beautiful, gentle bull, he swam out of the sea to greet them. Europa stroked him, fed him with flowers, and wound garlands round his neck. Then she set off across the sea with him. Her friends never saw her again. Zeus took Europa to the island of Crete, where they had three sons. Europa's story is remembered today in the name of the continent of Europe.

▲ MY HERO!

Perseus supports Andromeda with a steady arm as he plucks her from a fierce sea monster. According to Greek myths, Andromeda was the daughter of an African king. Her father boasted that she was more beautiful than the sea-nymphs. This made the nymphs' father, the sea god Poseidon, angry. He sent floods and a sea monster to attack the king's lands. They would only go away if Andromeda was killed as a sacrifice. Reluctantly, her parents left her on the shore to be eaten by the beast. She was rescued just in time by Perseus, who later married her.

▲ THE HUNCHBACK OF NOTRE DAME

French writer Victor Hugo's best-selling novel, published in 1831, tells the story of Quasimodo, a hunchbacked bell-ringer who works in the cathedral of Notre Dame (Our Lady), Paris. Quasimodo falls in love with Esmeralda, a gypsy girl who seeks refuge in the cathedral. He is bewitched by her beauty, and tries to protect her from her enemies. At first, Esmeralda is frightened by Quasimodo's appearance, but she is grateful for his kindness, and becomes fond of him. The story has a tragic end when the cathedral is attacked and Quasimodo falls to his death from the bell-tower.

▲ MUSIC AND MAGIC HERBS

Circe was a beautiful witch who turned people into animals. She lived on a remote island, where the Greek hero Odysseus arrived by chance with his men. They heard Circe's beautiful singing and were irresistibly drawn towards her home in a forest cave. Some of the men went inside, where Circe welcomed them graciously. When they woke up the next morning, she had turned them all into pigs. Odysseus vowed to save them. With the help of a magic herb to protect him, he made Circe fall in love with him. Then he persuaded her to turn all his men back into their own shape.

▲ BEAUTY AND THE BEAST

Beauty sits down to an uncomfortable meal with the Beast. The story of Beauty and the Beast was first written in Italy about 500 years ago. It has been retold many times since then. In the story, Beauty had to live with the Beast to save her father. Although she was very frightened, she made friends with the Beast and the Beast fell in love with her. When she agreed to marry him, the Beast was transformed into a handsome prince!

WILD SWANS ▶

Eleven wild swans, bewitched by a wicked stepmother, turn back into young men. Danish story-teller Hans Christian Andersen told how the evil stepmother changed eleven brothers into swans and threw their sister out of the house. A mysterious old woman told the sister what to do. She had to make each brother a shirt of stinging nettles and could not speak a word, however much the nettles hurt her hands as she sewed. The sister did as she was told, even though a handsome prince fell in love with her and wanted to help her. At last, the shirts were finished. She put them on each of the swans, and they became her brothers once more. She was able to speak to the prince, and told him she loved him, too.

Travellers' Tales

Explorers have brought back many stories of monsters from far-away lands. Some of these monsters were based on local myths and legends that travellers heard on their journeys. In North American forests, native people told travellers to beware of the hairy ape-man Bigfoot. In Australia, Aboriginal people warned settlers against spirits such as the Yowie and hippopotamus-like Bunyip.

Some monsters may have been invented by local people playing a joke on visitors. Unbelievable creatures included the Phanesii of northern Europe, who were reported to have huge ears that they wrapped around themselves to keep warm, and the Blemyae of North Africa, who had faces in their chests and no heads at all. Some monsters, such as the Himalayan Yeti, may be based on real creatures seen at a distance or in strange surroundings.

Travellers' tales are good entertainment. Often, they serve a purpose, too. They let travellers portray themselves as brave, adventurous heroes. They also allow them to praise or find fault with their own society by comparing it with other places they have seen.

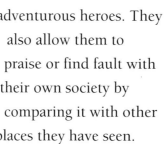

▲ **SHADED FROM THE SUN**
A Sciapod uses his outsized foot like an umbrella, to shelter his face from the Sun. According to ancient Greek and Roman writers, Sciapods were naked, man-shaped creatures who hopped about on one leg that ended in an enormous foot. They lived in India, and were shy and highly sensitive to sunlight. The Italian traveller Marco Polo, who set off in 1271 to explore many lands in Asia, claimed to have seen Sciapods, as well as men with heads like dogs who lived on islands off the Indian coast.

▲ **MOUNTAIN MONSTER**
The Yowie was a tall, hairy spirit with fierce long fangs. He guarded a mountain in south-east Australia called Jaal Gunboon or Mount Lindsay. Aboriginal people told newly arrived settlers in Australia that the Yowie would not harm humans unless they set foot on the mountain, or took sticks and stones away from it. If anyone dared to trespass on the mountain, the Yowie would attack.

◀ **ABOMINABLE SNOWMAN**
In 1925, explorers visiting the mighty Himalayan mountains on the borders of India, Nepal, China and Tibet brought back news of the Yeti, or Abominable Snowman. They claimed to have glimpsed one of these large, hairy apes from only 300m away, and to have seen giant footprints in the snow. Local people said Yetis had been sighted in the mountains for many hundreds of years. They were usually peaceful creatures, but sometimes they attacked lone travellers or shepherd girls. Scientists still do not know what Yetis are. They think they may be a kind of ape or the Himalayan Blue Bear.

▲ GULLIVER'S TRAVELS

Even though it is he who is normal-sized, Gulliver appears to be a giant compared to the tiny citizens of Lilliput. This imaginary country was created by Irish author Jonathan Swift, who lived from 1667 to 1745. Swift's best-selling book, *Gulliver's Travels*, is a satire (it makes fun of the way people behave). In Swift's book, Gulliver visits Brobdingnag, the land of giants, Lilliput, the land of little people, Laputa, the land of scientists and magicians, and Houyhnhnmland, a country run by wise, gentle horses. The horses govern rude, dirty, brutal Yahoos, who were how Swift saw ordinary men and women of his time.

▲ DESERT DJINN

Two merchants meet a terrifying, giant-sized djinn (genie). Travellers in the deserts of Arabia or Central Asia always feared seeing a djinn. These wilderness spirits could take any shape they chose. They could find pathways into mysterious otherworlds, and fly on magic carpets. Djinns could also conjure up fresh water, ripe fruits and beautiful palaces in the desert. They would suddenly vanish, leaving travellers lost and forlorn.

PRESENTED TO THE POPE ▶

This strange sea-monster is shaped like a lion but covered in scales like a fish. According to old chronicles (lists of important events) it was found on a beach in southern Italy around AD1535, and had the voice of a man. It was captured and taken to Rome to be presented to the Pope. We do not know for certain, but it is possible that if the Pope had looked very carefully, he might have found nothing more than a man inside a sea-monster costume.

Moving Monster Model

Tritons were Greek mermen – half fish, half human. A triton guided the ship belonging to the Greek hero Jason back home after he had stolen the Golden Fleece from a dragon. But other tritons attacked humans. One lived near the Greek town of Tanagra. Every day, it swam ashore to seize people or cattle. In the end, the Tanagrans left a bowl of wine out for the triton. He drank it all, then collapsed on the sand, fast asleep. Before he could wake up again, they cut off his head!

You can make a model of triton in this project, based on stone statues of this Greek monster.

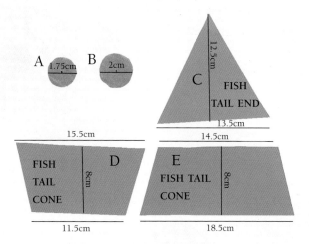

1 Use the compasses to draw templates A and B on cardboard. Cut them out.. Use the compasses to make a hole in the centre of each one. Copy C, D and E on the stiff coloured paper and cut them out.

You will need: modelling clay, cutting board, pair of compasses, scissors, cardboard, stiff coloured paper, thin coloured paper 5cm diameter polystyrene ball, sculpting or modelling tool, sticky tape, PVA glue, (including gold and silver), large needle, elastic thread, paint, paintbrushes.

6 Curve templates C, D and E as shown, and glue together the edges of each one. You have three cone shapes. The one from template C has a pointed end.

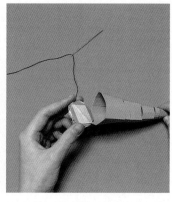

7 Thread elastic through the hole in template A. Tape the end on the underside to secure. Glue the circle into cone C about 1cm from the wide end.

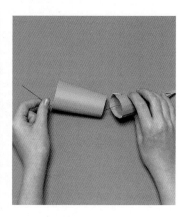

8 Draw the elastic up through cones C and D, from the narrow to wide ends. The narrow end of D fits into the open end of C. Do the same with cone E.

Tritons had the head and body of a man and, below the waist, a thick, muscular, coiling tail covered with shiny scales. They used their tails to swim and to leap above the waves. Each triton carried a large conch shell, which he blew like a trumpet. A single blast of sound was said to calm stormy seas.

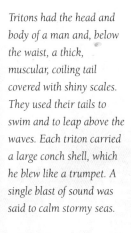

11 Cut 5 strips of thin paper measuring 1.5cm in width. Cut small triangles out of the strips to make scales for the monster's tail.

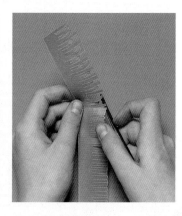

12 Cut a strip of thin paper measuring 2cm in width and make small cuts along it for hair. Curve the thin cuts over the edge of a sculpting tool.

2 Make a clay rectangle measuring 10 x 5cm for the body. Use extra clay to attach a polystyrene ball to the back of the rectangle.

3 Roll out two sausage shapes of clay, each about 1cm thick, for arms. Wet the clay a little with water to attach the arms to the sides of body, as shown.

4 Attach a small ball of clay to the body for the head. Add details to the body and face using a sculpting or modelling tool, as shown.

5 To make the tail, fold template C in half. Make seven small cuts along the folded edge. Make the cuts gradually smaller towards the point.

9 Thread the elastic through the hole in template B. Fit B into the end of the cone. Make a cut in the edge of cone E. Pull the elastic through it to secure.

10 Cover the end of the clay figure (the portion with the polystyrene ball inside it) with PVA glue. Insert it into the end of the card tube.

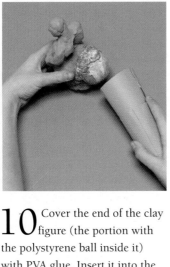

13 Glue the paper strips of scales around the tail. Make sure you do not cover the joints because you want them to be able to move around.

14 Paint the clay figure. Glue on the hair, and gold and silver decorations to the tail. Paint detail on the monster's face and body.

Your model's tail will bend and sway easily – just like that of the original triton. According to Greek mythology, these creatures were the sons of the sea god Poseidon and the sea nymph Amphitrite.

Weird Weapons

Monsters are always fighting! They attack humans and each other, and are often attacked by humans in return. Many of the fiercest creatures are equipped with in-built weapons, such as sharp teeth or claws. Some carry fearsome arms, such as the tridents (three-pronged forks) wielded by many sea-monsters. A few frail, ghostly spirits, such as the beautiful Villis who lived in dark European forests, use energy from human victims as a weapon. They lure young men to dance all night long until they drop dead from exhaustion. Many fiends use magic spells or curses to do harm.

Monsters are difficult to defeat. Most are bigger and stronger than humans and often have magic powers. Anyone who wants to defeat them has to use cunning or trickery, or rely on supernatural powers. Only the bravest heroes, or a person helped by the gods, succeed.

▲ FIRE-BREATHER

An angry dragon breathes out a huge tongue of flame. In Europe and the Middle East, dragons were evil, greedy and dangerous. They were a sign of awesome, destructive power. Some were thought to be devils. Whenever they crawled out of their lairs, in caves or rocks, their fiery breath scorched the countryside all around. It also burned up any person who dared approach them without taking special care.

◄ DEADLY SONGS

Sirens were female sea creatures who lured sailors to their doom by singing songs of incredible sweetness. According to ancient Greek stories, the Sirens lived on a rocky island and sang whenever a ship sailed past. Sailors could not resist them – they were forced to steer straight towards them. Many ships were smashed to pieces on the rocks and their crews were drowned. Sailors who survived and reached the island found that they could not move. They simply sat and listened to the Sirens' singing until they died from hunger and thirst. As a result, the Sirens' island was covered in heaps of skin and bones.

▲ A BULLET THROUGH THE HEART

The only defence against a werewolf is a gun loaded with silver bullets. Werewolves (men who become wolves at full Moon) are almost impossible to kill. Only a silver bullet through the heart is said to work. Silver defeats evil because it is a symbol of purity, hope and the Moon. Silver bullets use the Moon's power to defeat creatures that depend on moonlight to survive.

▲ KILLED BY THE CROSS

According to Christian legends, Saint Margaret of Antioch (in present-day Turkey) was swallowed by a dragon, which was really the devil in disguise. But Margaret did not despair. She made the sign of the cross, the most holy Christian symbol. Miraculously, the dragon split open, and Margaret stepped out from its swollen stomach. In the Middle Ages (around AD1000–1500), Margaret was honoured as a saint. Pregnant women asked for her help to make sure that their babies would be born safely.

◀ BELOW THE NET

The Persian giant Zammurad peers out from the well where he has been trapped under a net. In many countries, nets were mysterious and magical weapons. It seemed extraordinary that something so full of holes could be used as a container and that something so light and flimsy-looking could be so strong. This picture of Zammurad was painted for the Mughal rulers of India in the 1500s. It was an illustration from a collection of famous Persian tales.

SKY-WALKERS ▶

A dakini waves a fearsome curved knife and carries a skull-cup filled with blood. She stands ready to protect the spirits of holy men and women. Dakini were Buddhist guardian goddesses from Tibet, where they were known as *mkah-hgro* (sky-walkers). They were always portrayed with deadly weapons, skull necklaces and fierce expressions. Buddhist worshippers left them offerings, to ensure their good will.

▲ KNIGHT IN SHINING ARMOUR

A valiant knight named George aims a deadly blow at an ugly dragon who has captured a woman. The dragon has been terrorizing a local village by feasting on its population. The woman is to be his latest meal – until, by chance, George arrives on his horse. To defeat this cruel monster, George skewers its belly with a lance (a long spear). This causes the dragon to spit a jet of flame straight at him. So George stabs and slices, and then, with one mighty blow, he cuts off the dragon's head. In the Middle Ages, the story of George and the dragon was very popular, and he came to be the patron saint of England.

Mighty Sword and Shield

No brave hero or knight should be without his trusty sword and shield. They are essential in the fight against monsters. In this project, you can make your own sword and shield.

The legendary King Arthur wielded a sword known as Excalibur. With this mighty blade, Arthur drove out monsters and giants from ancient Britain.

Shields were not just used for defence. The Greek hero Perseus used his shield to help him kill Medusa. People believed that the shiny surfaces of shields gave them magical powers. They also felt that the special patterns on some shields made them magic.

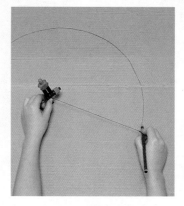

1 Tie a piece of string about 22cm long to a pencil and a pair of compasses, as shown. Draw a circle with a radius of 22cm on to cardboard. Cut out.

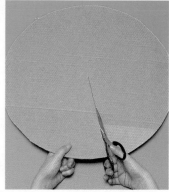

2 Take the cardboard circle and, using a pair of scissors, make a cut in to the centre. This will allow you to slightly curve the cardboard circle.

You will need: string, pair of compasses, pencil, 2 large pieces of thick cardboard measuring at least 44 x 44cm, scissors, PVA glue, gold paper, silver paper, 5 pieces of thick cardboard measuring at least 12 x 8cm, 2 strips of thick cardboard measuring 3 x 25cm, sticky tape, piece of thick cardboard measuring 15 x 30cm, black paint, paintbrush, silver foil.

7 Cut out the inner circle in stages with scissors, as shown. Ask an adult to help you. This will leave you with a ring of cardboard.

8 Cut through the ring of cardboard in one place using scissors, as shown. Now cover the ring in silver paper. Wrap the paper around and glue it down.

9 Glue the silver ring on to the edge of the gold shield. You will have to overlap the ends of the silver disc and glue them down too, as shown.

Many soldiers tried to attack Medusa with their swords, but they all turned to stone as soon as she looked at them. Perseus was cleverer. He waited until Medusa was asleep, then crept up behind her. He did not look at her directly, but watched her reflection in his shiny shield – then sliced off her head.

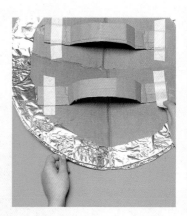

12 Take the strips of thick cardboard measuring 3 x 25cm. Curve the strips. Glue and tape them on the back of your shield to make handles.

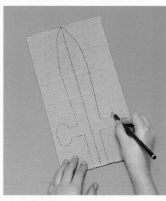

13 Take the rectangle of thick cardboard measuring 15 x 30cm. Draw a line down the centre as a guide. Draw the shape of a sword.

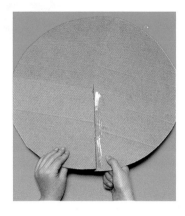

3 Line the edges of the cut you have made in the circle with glue. Overlap the edges by 2cm and stick them together, so your shield is curved.

4 Place the card circle on top of a piece of gold paper. Draw a circle 2cm larger than the card circle, as shown. Now cut out this gold circle.

5 Glue the gold circle on to your cardboard circle. Turn over and make small cuts along the edges. Fold the edges over the circle and glue, as shown.

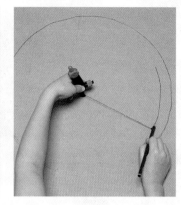

6 Set the compasses at 22cm and draw another circle on to thick card. Now draw a smaller circle inside it. This smaller circle should have a radius of 20cm.

10 Draw a tear shape measuring about 12 x 8cm on to thick card. Cut out the tear shape and make four others using the first as a template.

11 Cover three of the tear shapes in silver paper and two in gold paper. Glue the tear shapes on to the gold shield, keeping them evenly spaced.

Greek swords were mostly short, single-edged blades made of iron. They were used for close hand-to-hand fighting. Sometimes blades were curved, but more often they were straight and broad. Although Greek swords were usually left undecorated, some had handles made of bone.

14 Cut out the sword shape from the cardboard. Now, paint the handle with black paint. (Remember to paint both sides of the handle!)

15 Finally, cover both sides of the blade in silver foil. Use PVA glue to stick the silver foil to the blade. Now you have a sword with a shiny surface.

Real-life Wonders

The natural world is full of amazing creatures. Many can seem quite monstrous or frightening. But the oddest looking animals or plants are in fact just well suited to survival in their surroundings. For example, the pitcher plant traps and eats slugs and frogs because the soil in which it grows does not have enough goodness in it to nourish the plant. Some beautiful lilies smell of rotting meat to attract insects carrying pollen that will fertilize their flowers. Deep-sea fish glow in the dark because no sunlight can reach the ocean floor.

People, animals or plants that do not develop normally, or are affected by disease, are regarded by some people as monsters. In the past, people with unusual bodies, such as Siamese twins, were put on display. Today, we think that is wrong. We aim to treat everyone with equal respect.

▲ PUT ON DISPLAY

A fairground spectator stares in horror at John Merrick, the so-called Elephant Man. Merrick, born in 1862, suffered from a rare disease that produced lumpy skin and thickened, distorted bones, and which left him with severe breathing difficulties. Instead of receiving proper treatment, he was put on show in a fairground. Eventually, Merrick's head became so heavy that his neck could not support its weight and he died in his sleep at hospital in 1890, aged 28.

▲ BIGGEST BEETLE?

With huge mandibles (mouth-parts) stretched out in front of it, a Hercules beetle lumbers across the forest floor. The Hercules beetle is Europe's largest beetle. An adult can measure about 5cm long. Its ferocious mandibles help it to chomp through food it finds in the forest. Like all beetles, the Hercules beetle has folding wings, protected by elytra (hard, shiny wing-cases) and large, compound eyes, each made up of thousands of separate lenses.

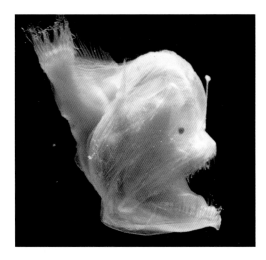

▲ LIGHT IN THE DARK

An angler fish swims in search of prey, glowing eerily like a ghost. A luminous lure floats above its huge, fierce jaws like an angler's bait. The lure is part of its body, and attracts smaller fish towards it, so they can be snapped up and eaten. The light is produced by millions of glowing bacteria, which live in the lure. Other deep-sea fish have special chemicals in their cells. When combined with oxygen, these chemicals glow in the dark.

▲ GOGGLE-EYED, EIGHT-LEGGED

A deep-sea diver is dwarfed by a giant octopus. Its trailing tentacles (legs) measure about 10m. Most octopuses are small. They rarely grow to more than 1m long. Over 150 different species of octopus live in the oceans. All have eight tentacles and huge goggle eyes, and are carnivores (meat-eaters). They catch prey in their tentacles, which direct it to their huge, beak-like mouths. There, the prey is injected with poison from salivary glands.

◀ TRAPPED BY A DEADLY PLANT

The Venus flytrap finds the food it needs by trapping flies and other insects between fast-closing parts of its leaves, called lobes. Each lobe is fringed by fine hairs, which act as triggers. The moment a creature lands on them, the trigger-hairs release a chemical messenger, telling the lobes to snap shut. The creature is trapped inside, where it is slowly digested by more chemicals given off by the lobes. The nourishment it contains is absorbed by cells in the plant.

FLESH-EATER ▶

Pitcher plants drown unlucky insects and small creatures before eating them. Their leaves are shaped like hollow containers, such as pitchers or jugs. They are filled with a special liquid. When insects crawl inside the leaf, they fall into the liquid. They soon become waterlogged and cannot escape. Their bodies are dissolved by special enzymes (chemicals) in the liquid, and the nourishment they contain is absorbed by the plant. Some pitcher plants are big enough to trap frogs, slugs and small birds.

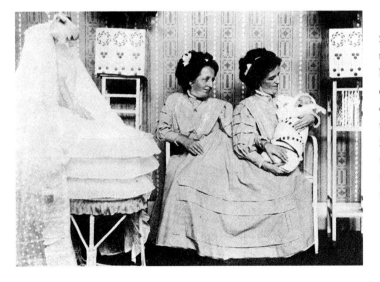

◀ TOGETHER FOR LIFE

Siamese twins Rosa and Josepha Blazek sit with Josepha's baby. Siamese twins are born joined together, usually at the hip, chest, abdomen (lower body) or head. Like other identical twins, they are formed when a fertilized egg splits in two inside a mother's womb. Usually, the egg divides completely, but with Siamese twins, the two parts remain joined. Siamese twins get their name from Chang and Eng, twins from Thailand (formerly Siam), who lived from 1811 to 1874. In the past, people regarded Siamese twins and other people with unusual bodies as so different that people had the right to display them to others for a price. Until recently, separation was impossible but now surgeons often succeed in separating Siamese twins.

GIANT'S FOOTSTEPS! ▶

Like a walkway built for giants, these stone columns stretch for hundreds of metres along the coast of County Antrim, Northern Ireland. People once believed that they were part of a huge pathway made by a giant so that he could walk across the sea from Ireland to Scotland, where there are similar rock formations. In fact, the 'causeway' was made naturally about 12 million years ago by volcanic rock. Each column measures about 50cm across. The tallest is 6m high. Just right for giant's steps!

Monsters in Art

Monsters are popular subjects for many works of art. For centuries, they have appeared in paintings, books and plays. Sometimes, these works have carried a religious or moral message (showing people how to behave better). Sometimes they have had a political purpose, or have been designed to make people think. Fearsome images and stories have also been used to explore people's innermost minds, and their dreams, hopes and fears.

During the 20th century, monsters, from creepy vampires to aliens from space, featured in many films. Clever camerawork and special effects made it possible to show extraordinary creatures on screen, alongside real people. Film-makers also made good use of vivid colours, loud sounds and rapid movements to create life-like feelings of horror and excitement. Today, computer, console and Internet games feature monsters of many different kinds. Players use their wits and skills to fight a new generation of monsters.

▲ DOUBLE IDENTITY

The murderous Mr Hyde lurks in a dark alleyway with his cane raised, ready to strike an innocent passer-by. Soon, he will turn back into Dr Jekyll, a kindly, respectable medical man. People have been fascinated by the idea of one person with two identities ever since Robert Louis Stevenson wrote *The Strange Case of Dr Jekyll and Mr Hyde* in 1886. His book tells how, by taking a special medicine, the good scientist Jekyll could transform himself into the evil Hyde whenever he chose.

THE DAY OF THE TRIFFIDS ▶

A giant plant attacks actress Janette Scott in *The Day of the Triffids*, a film made in 1962. The original story was written by English author John Wyndham. In it, lethal and aggressive plant monsters, called triffids, invaded Earth and tried to take over. Triffids were massive – mostly over 2m high. They moved around on three-pronged roots. Now, we use the word triffid to describe any kind of imaginary hostile and dangerous plant. John Wyndham intended his story to be a warning to people about how they might react to big changes in the world.

◀ MONSTERS IN THE MIND

A monster squats on the chest of a woman, trying to suffocate her, while a wild-eyed horse peers through the bedroom curtains. Is the horse going to speak, or attack? This strange picture was painted by the Swiss artist Henry Fuseli (1741–1825). It shows a young woman having a nightmare. Fuseli has tried to show the fear and confusion in the woman's mind, caused by her strange dream. Almost everyone has nightmares at some time in their life. They are most common in children and teenagers, but rare among old people.

▲ KING OF THE MONSTERS

Godzilla, a mighty lizard-like creature more than 100m high, has been called the king of the monsters. He began life in Japan in 1954, and was created by film-maker Eiji Tsuburaya. In Japanese, his name was Gojira. The first Godzilla film in English appeared in 1956. Since then, there have been many more films, all very popular worldwide. Godzilla's huge size was due to exposure to atomic radiation. At first, Godzilla was meant to symbolize the terrible power of atomic weapons, and how they threaten humanity. (Japan is the only country to have been attacked by atom bombs, in 1945.) Later films show Godzilla fighting aliens from far-away planets, other monsters, genetically-engineered creatures, robots and pollution.

◀ ALIENS!

This is a model of an adult monster from the film *Alien* (directed by Ridley Scott in 1979). People have been fascinated by science-fiction monsters for more than a hundred years. In *Alien*, monsters' eggs hatch into larvae (young) called facehuggers. They attach themselves to a human victim, and plant the seed for an adult alien. When it is grown, the alien bursts out of the human's body.

▲ VISIONS OF HELL

Devils, monsters and all kinds of nightmare creatures torment dead people in this picture of Hell. It was painted by Dutch artist Hieronymus Bosch, who lived from about 1450 to 1516. As a sincere Christian, he believed that Hell was a place where sinful people went after death. There, they were punished for all the wrong and wicked things they had done while they were alive. Historians have suggested that Bosch based his terrifying picture on other monster images he might have seen, such as gargoyles on cathedral roofs, or strange beasts painted in the borders of medieval manuscripts.

Frankenstein Monster Mask

Ever since Frankenstein's monster appeared in print in 1818, he has captured imaginations everywhere, perhaps because his story is not only spine-chilling but tragic, too. The monster is a huge, lumbering, almost-human creature, created from dead flesh and brought to life by a young science student called Frankenstein. Although Frankenstein's monster looks awkward and ugly, he is good-natured, at least at first. But when his creator refuses to treat him like other people, or to care for him, the monster's peaceful feelings change to hatred and violence.

1 Blow up the balloon. Soak newspaper strips with the glue mix to make papier-mâché. Cover one side of the balloon with 4 layers and allow to dry.

2 When the papier-mâché is completely dry, burst the balloon. Remove the papier-mâché and trim around edges to produce a rounded face mask.

You will need: *round balloon, papier-mâché mix (half water, half PVA glue), paintbrushes, scissors, pieces of thick cardboard (29 x 14cm, 22 x 12cm, 29 x 9.5cm, plus other scraps), ruler, pencil, pair of compasses, PVA glue, brown gum tape, masking tape, 2 balsa dowels (3cm long, 0.5cm diameter), paints in black and other colours, string or elastic.*

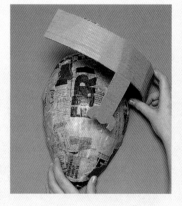

7 Cover the back of the head and nose piece with PVA glue. Then stick it in position on top of the papier-mâché face mask, as shown.

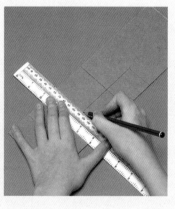

8 Draw a line in the centre of the 29 x 9.5cm cardboard. Draw a 4 x 10cm rectangle at the centre of the line, touching the bottom edge of card. Cut it out.

9 Cover the back of the cardboard jaw piece with PVA glue. Carefully stick it into position over the lower part of the mask, as shown.

The story of Frankenstein has been made into many films over the years. Today, it is often seen as a warning about what might happen if scientists rush ahead with experiments without thinking about what the results might be.

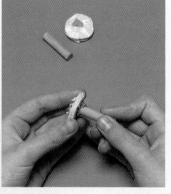

12 Make a hole in the centre of each cardboard circle with the end of scissors. Push the balsa dowel through the middle. Glue in position and paint black.

13 Paint your mask with a base colour first (for example, grey-green). Wait for that to dry and then paint in details using other colours.

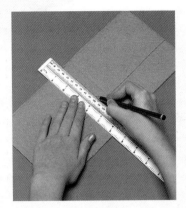

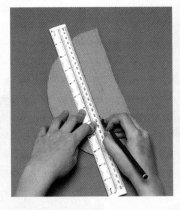

3 Take the cardboard rectangle measuring 29 x 14cm. Draw a pencil line 5cm from the long edge. Then draw a pencil line across the middle, as shown.

4 Draw the shape of a nose with the centre line in the middle. Make the nose 3cm wide on the bridge and 6cm at the nostril. Cut out nose and brow.

5 Set a pair of compasses at 11cm and draw a semicircle on thick card. Cut it out. Draw a pencil line 5cm from the straight edge. Cut the 5cm piece off.

6 Line the edges of the semicircle of card with PVA glue and stick it to the top edge of the nose piece, as shown. Hold together until the glue has dried.

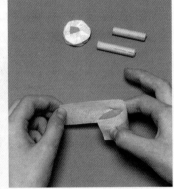

10 Cover the gaps between the stuck-on face parts and the papier-mâché face mask with brown gum tape. This will make sure the face parts stay on.

11 Set a pair of compasses at 1cm and draw two circles on some cardboard. Cut them out and cover in masking tape. Take the two balsa dowels.

To finish your mask, tie or tape string or elastic on either side of the mask. If you can find some old clothes, such as an old shirt, you could decorate them as well, perhaps with gruesome blood stains made with red paint.

14 Wait for the paint on the mask to dry completely. Then push the balsa-dowel bolts through either side of the forehead and glue in place.

15 Place the mask over your face and guess where the eyeholes should be. Take the mask off and make eyeholes using the scissors, as shown.

▲ No, No, GMO!

Demonstrators dressed in protective clothing destroy a trial crop of genetically modified oilseed rape in Britain. In the late 1990s, protests against the introduction of GMOs (genetically modified organisms) increased throughout Europe. Although scientists and governments argued that GMOs were safe, members of the public did not agree. Some people did not want to eat genetically-modified food, and many worry that 'rogue' genes from trial plantings of GMOs might escape and interbreed with normal crops and wild plants.

Modern Monsters

Some people say that we are creating new monsters today. They believe that we are letting science run out of control, by breeding new kinds of crops and animals in unnatural ways. They argue that we are dangerously close to breaking down the natural barriers between humanity and other animal species, and between humans and machines. There are fears that medical technology based on genetics will create monstrous creatures that are part-animal, part-human, and that, before long, cyborgs (mixtures of men and machines) will be walking around. Some people suggest that in the future, robots will be able to think, and may outwit their builders, becoming mechanical monsters with awesome powers. Many environmental campaigners also worry about the pollution caused by modern science.

Not everyone agrees with this view. Many regard medical and genetic research as a way of curing serious diseases, such as diabetes and cystic fibrosis. They claim genetically-modified crops will help end world hunger, and that future science will create not monsters, but a better, safer world.

▲ Hello Dolly!

She looks just like any other sheep. But Dolly, born in 1997 at the Roslin Institute in Scotland, was the first mammal cloned (copied) from adult cells. Normally, mammals reproduce by combining egg cells from a female and sperm cells from a male. Dolly was produced by taking cells from an adult female sheep and removing the DNA (the chemical instructions for life) from them. This was put into another sheep's egg cell from which the DNA had been removed. The new egg cell was then put inside a mother sheep, where it grew into a lamb in the normal way.

ROCK ROBOT ▶

A Japanese robot plays keyboards in a 1990s rock band. The first working robot was designed by British inventor C.W. Kenward in 1957. The idea soon spread to the United States, where robots were used in car factories to assemble the vehicles. A robot with human-like arms, used to paint objects, was made in Norway in 1966. Since then, many robots capable of precise, delicate movements have been built, especially in Japan.

◀ INVISIBLE THREAT

Warning flags mark the boundary of the power station at Chernobyl, Ukraine, site of the world's worst nuclear accident. It happened in 1986, when a nuclear reactor became dangerously overheated, releasing clouds of invisible radioactive particles into the air. They were spread by the wind across Russia and Europe like a silent, deadly monster. This pollution killed many workers at the power station, and has caused serious illnesses among thousands of people living nearby. Doctors fear that it will also lead to an increase in deaths from cancer in all the areas affected by the pollution for the next 20–30 years.

▲ MEDICAL MOUSE

It looks like something from science fiction, but this mouse with a human ear growing on its back is science fact. In 1995, doctors at the University of Massachussetts perfected a new technique, called tissue engineering. It allowed them to 'grow' new ears, noses and other human body parts to replace ones that had been damaged in accidents or by disease. This ear-shaped piece of human tissue was grown on the back of a mouse that had been specially bred not to reject it. Such tissue can be used as spare parts for humans.

▲ COMING TO A SCREEN NEAR YOU

Today, snarling monsters and bloodthirsty creatures are fought all the time by millions of ordinary people in computer games. Many nasties from the past appear in computer games, such as the living dead and one-eyed Cyclops, as well as a whole new range of monsters. Many people now play games over the Internet, with a number of people on separate computers competing with each other in the same game. Computer game tournaments are held around the world, and gaming champions may one day become as famous as today's sporting heroes or the mythical, dragon-slaying heroes of the past!

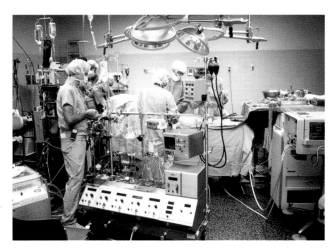

▲ HEART TO HEART

Doctors transplant a pig's heart valve into a human patient, whose own valve has failed. Although pigs look very different to humans, many parts of their bodies are surprisingly similar. Carefully sterilized (cleaned) valves from pigs' hearts have been used since the 1980s to help repair damaged human ones. In the late 1990s, scientists talked of transplanting cells from humans into pigs, so that pigs' organs could be modified to use as human spare parts. Many people believe it is dangerous to mix human and animal cells.

Timeline

For thousands of years, people have enjoyed monster stories. Monsters can be silly, spectacular, strange or scary. They can help us cope with secret fears, and explain things we cannot understand. They warn us about dangers, encourage us to obey – or break – society's rules, and make us think. But most of all, monsters are fun!

65million–50,000BC

65 million years ago THE LAST DINOSAURS roam the Earth. Fossilized dinosaur bones, found millions of years later, may have led to people believing in unseen, gigantic monsters. There are also sightings of dinosaur-like monsters today, such as the Mokele-Mbembe from the Congo in Central Africa.

50,000BC ABORIGINAL PEOPLE settle in Australia. Aboriginal Dreamtime (creation) songs and stories describe the Australian landscape and many magical creatures and monsters.

Mokele-Mbembe

50,000–1500BC

3800–1028BC CRAFTWORKERS from the Liangzhu and Shang cultures in China decorate many jade and bronze objects with Taotie monsters (dead ancestors transformed into creatures with claws and horns).

3100–300BC ANCIENT EGYPTIAN CIVILIZATION Many Egyptian wall-paintings and Books of the Dead (guides to life after death) describe fierce monsters lurking in the Underworld (known as Duat).

2000–1450BC MINOAN PEOPLE living on the Greek island of Crete honour the bull-headed Minotaur monster, which lives in a maze called the labyrinth.

AD1–AD500

1–600 NAZCA PEOPLE OF PERU create vast images of strange animals and monsters in the desert. Strangely, they can only properly be seen from the air.

300–900 MAYA PEOPLE of south-east Mexico, Guatemala and Belize summon the spirits of their dead ancestors in the shape of snake-monsters by offering sacrifices of blood.

432 ACCORDING TO LEGEND, Saint Patrick uses prayer to drive all snakes out of Ireland.

Loch Ness Monster

AD500–800

565 FIRST RECORDED SIGHTING OF THE LOCH NESS Monster in Scotland. Saint Columba buries a man reported to have been bitten to death by the monster.

800–1100 IN NORTHERN EUROPE, Iceland and Greenland, Viking people decorate jewellery, buildings and stone monuments with patterns of fantastic creatures. Viking stories and religious myths also describe many monsters.

800–1150 AT TULA in Mexico, the Toltec people carve chac-mool monsters to contain human hearts and blood offered as sacrifices to their gods.

AD800–1000

800s–1400s TRADITIONAL FOLK TALES from Middle Eastern lands are written down in a collection of stories known as the *Arabian Nights*. Among the many fantastic creatures in the stories are djinns (genies) and giant birds called rocs.

Grendel

900 SAXON POEM *BEOWULF* features a terrifying swamp-monster called Grendel.

1400–1500

A mermaid

1450s EUROPEAN ARTISTS decorate many of their works with grotesques (peculiar-looking creatures that are part-human, part-animal).

1450–1516 DUTCH ARTIST Hieronymus Bosch paints pictures of Hell crowded with terrifying demons and monsters.

1493–1541 SWISS SCHOLAR PARACELSUS describes sylphs, beautiful, human-like creatures without souls that inhabit the air.

1500–1600

c.1500–1600 THE STORY OF *BEAUTY AND THE BEAST* is first written down in Italy.

1519–1522 SHIP BELONGING TO PORTUGUESE EXPLORER Ferdinand Magellan makes the first voyage right round the world. Many explorers after him tell of strange sea monsters encountered on their travels.

1535 A STRANGE SEA-MONSTER shaped like a lion but covered with the scales of a fish is presented to the Pope in Rome.

sea monster

1600–1700

1600 onwards JEWISH FOLK-TALES tell of dybbuks, demons that take possession of people and speak through them.

1600–1850 NATIVE AMERICAN PEOPLES who live as nomads on the Great Plains honour a spirit known as the Thunderbird, which brings dangerous storms or welcome rain.

1690 THE STORY OF *LITTLE RED RIDING HOOD* is written down for the first time.

1830–1850

1841 THE BALLET *GISELLE*, created by Adolphe Adam, features Villis, spirits that look like beautiful women. They lure young men to dance with them and keep them dancing until they die from exhaustion.

Giselle

1850–1900

Late 1800s JOHN MERRICK was born with a rare genetic disease that affected the growth of his bones. He was exhibited in many popular shows in England and became known as The Elephant Man.

1886 ROBERT LOUIS STEVENSON writes *The Strange Case of Dr Jekyll and Mr Hyde*, the story of a doctor who discovers a medicine that changes him into an evil monster called Mr Hyde.

Mr Hyde

1900–1930

1921 EXPLORERS IN THE HIMALAYA MOUNTAINS OF TIBET bring back the first reports of Yetis (huge, hairy monsters) to Europe. Tibetan people say Yetis had been seen in the mountains for hundreds of years previously.

Yeti

1500–1000BC

1500BC ARYAN PEOPLE arrive in northern India from Central Asia. Their stories, myths and legends describe many gods, demons and monsters.

1500BC–AD200 THE OLMEC PEOPLE of Central America create carved 'were-jaguar' figures. These carvings show humans, including babies, turning into creatures with fierce jaguar-like fangs.

1450BC THE BABYLONIAN MYTH *Enuma Elish* tells how god-hero Marduk kills a two-headed dragon, called Tiamat. From her body, he creates the earth, sea and sky.

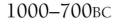
Medusa

1000–700BC

1000–300BC MANY STRANGE AND WONDERFUL monsters feature in ancient Greek myths and legends, and also in ancient Greek plays, poems and art.

800BC–AD100 CELTIC PEOPLES IN EUROPE portray animal monsters in their art.

750BC–AD400 ANCIENT ROMANS continue Greek monster traditions, and add many new creatures of their own.

700BC IN GREEK MYTHOLOGY, natural sea hazards are described as monsters. Dangerous rocks are Scylla (a monster with huge teeth) and a whirlpool is Charybdis (a swallowing monster).

700BC–AD1

609–539BC BABYLONIAN ARTISTS use a monstrous winged bull as a symbol of royal power.

400BC–AD858 PICTS (a mysterious people who live in Scotland) create works of art featuring shape-changing animals and other monsters.

221BC SHI HUANGDI becomes the first emperor of China. Dragons become symbols of his power.

130BC THE BIBLE STORY of Daniel in the Lion's Den is probably first written down. It tells how Daniel poisoned a dragon that was worshipped as a god. Daniel was thrown into a cage of lions, where he survived, thanks to his faith in God.

winged bull

AD1000–1200

1000 onwards THE NATIVE AMERICAN Haida people of north-west North America carve huge totem poles, decorated with monstrous faces of ancestors and spirits, out of tall redwood trees.

1000–1500 THE MIDDLE AGES IN EUROPE. Many magical monsters, such as unicorns, are used to decorate medieval manuscripts, tapestries and stained glass.

WILD MEN, such as the old English Wodewose or Woodiwiss, are rumoured to live in woods and forests throughout the world.

AD1200–1300

1245–1521 AZTEC PEOPLE of Mexico honour Quetzalcoatl, a winged serpent, as their guardian god. They believe that one day Quetzalcoatl will return and bring the world to an end.

Aztec serpent monster

AD1300–1400

1300 ITALIAN TRADER AND EXPLORER MARCO POLO travels to China and South-east Asia to trade. He brings back reports of strange peoples, including men with dogs' heads. Polo also mentions sightings of the roc, a giant bird that drops rocks on sailors in the Indian Ocean, sinking their ships.

A roc

1700–1800

1726 IRISH WRITER JONATHAN SWIFT publishes *Gulliver's Travels*, a fantasy about a shipwrecked sailor who lands on a series of undiscovered islands inhabited by races of giants, miniature people and talking horses.

1794 BRITISH NOVELIST ANN RADCLIFFE (better known as Mrs Radcliffe) writes *The Mysteries of Udolpho*, a famous horror story. Around this time, 'gothic' novels about gloomy castles, gibbering ghosts and fearful monsters are very popular.

Gulliver's Travels

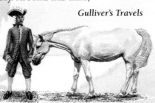

1800–1815

1800s–1900s FREAK SHOWS featuring people with physical differences, such as Siamese twins, are popular entertainment throughout Europe and the United States of America.

1800s–present PANTOMIMES are very popular with audiences in Europe. They are often based on folk-tales, such as *Jack the Giant Killer*.

1812–1815 MANY ANCIENT, traditional fairy stories and folk-tales from central Europe are collected by brothers Jacob and Wilhelm Grimm. These tales are then published in Germany.

Baba Yaga's house

AD1815–1830

1818 MARY SHELLEY'S novel *Frankenstein* is published. It tells of a medical student who creates a monster that he cannot control.

Frankenstein's monster

1930–1950

1931 A HORROR MOVIE BASED ON THE STORY OF *DRACULA* is made in Hollywood, United States. It features a blood-sucking vampire. In the same year, a film is made of Mary Shelley's novel *Frankenstein* (see 1815–1830 *above*).

1933 THE HORROR MOVIE *KING KONG* is made in Hollywood. It features a huge, gorilla-like monster that terrorizes New York City, United States.

1930s THE FIRST COLLECTION of photographs claiming to show the Loch Ness Monster are published. A scientific investigation of the monster begins.

Dracula

1950–1975

1954–1955 SCHOLAR AND WRITER J.R.R. TOLKEIN publishes his novel *The Lord of the Rings*. It tells of many strange creatures, both good and evil. The book soon attracts a huge cult following.

1955 THE JAPANESE MONSTER GODZILLA is first seen in films and books. This creature, which looks like the dinosaur Tyrannosaurus rex, looms over tall buildings and causes chaos wherever it goes.

1962 A FILM IS MADE of the novel *The Day of the Triffids*, in which giant plant monsters called triffids invade Earth.

1975–2000

1970s–1980s THE BOARD GAME *Dungeons and Dragons* becomes popular. It features many monsters and supernatural creatures.

1990s THE COMPUTER GAMES POKÉMON AND DIGIMON are invented in Japan. They feature monsters that fight each other, causing them to mutate (change) into different monsters with new skills and powers.

2000 THE YEAR OF THE DRAGON, according to the Chinese lunar (moon-based) calendar.

Chinese Dragon

GLOSSARY

abominable
Something greatly disliked or loathsome.

Ammut
An ancient Egyptian monster from the world of the dead. It was part crocodile, part lion and part hippo.

archaeologists
People who study the remains of the past.

atomic weapons
Powerful bombs that use the energy released when atoms (particles of matter) are destroyed to create vast explosions.

Aztec
A civilization in Mexico, central America, powerful from around AD1200–1530.

besotted
Deeply in love with someone.

Bunyip
A water-monster from Australia.

capsize
Turn over (a boat).

causeway
Raised road or path.

Celtic
Belonging to a civilization in Europe, powerful from around 800BC–AD100.

chac-mool
A container for hearts that were offered to the gods. Made by Aztec and other Central American peoples.

Chi Lin
A kindly, guardian monster from China.

chronicle
List of important events, year by year, in date order.

cloned
Copied by splitting off from a single parent, rather than by mating male and female.

cockatrice
An ancient Roman monster, a mixture of snake and cockerel.

conch shell
The hollow, spiral-shaped shell of a large sea-creature.

corn dolly
A model man or woman, made with straw at harvest time.

cyborgs
Monsters that are part human and part machine.

Cyclops
A one-eyed monster from ancient Greece.

dakini
Fierce guardian goddesses from Tibet, Asia.

djinn (or genie)
A spirit monster from deserts in Asia and the Middle East.

DNA
The chemical instructions for life, found inside all living cells.

enchant
To delight someone, or put a spell on them.

fabulous
(1) Wonderful (2) From a fable (story with a message).

fiend
A devil.

gamelan
An orchestra or a group of gongs played together, from Indonesia.

gargoyle
A horrid-looking face, with a gaping mouth, fixed to churches and other tall buildings.

genes
Tiny chemical messengers in human cells that pass on family likenesses, such as hair-colour, from parents to their children.

genetically modified organisms (GMOs)
Plants or animals that have had their genes modified (changed) by scientists.

Gorgons
Greek monsters who looked like beautiful women, with snakes instead of hair.

gnarled
Knobbly and twisted.

griffin
A bird monster from India and Central Asia. It had the head, wings and claws of an eagle, and the body of a lion.

hag
Ugly old woman.

harpy
A Greek or Roman goddess of wind and rain. They looked like birds with women's heads.

hide
Huge jellyfish sea monster from Chile.

husk
The rough outer casing of plant-seeds, such as wheat or maize.

Hydra
A huge snake monster with many heads, from ancient Greece.

Iroquois
Native people who lived in the north-east of North America.

kami
A frog-like water-monster, from Japan.

kraken
Huge sea-monster from Norwegian coast.

labyrinth (or maze)
A puzzling place with many confusing passages and turnings.

larvae
Young of insects and some monsters. They often look rather like worms.

Lorelei
A beautiful river-woman from Germany, who sang and lured men to their deaths.

luminous
Shining with its own light.

lunar
Relating to the moon.

lure
(1) To tempt a person or an animal into a trap. (2) Something used to attract prey.

manatee
A sea-mammal, rather like a large seal, that lives in warm waters.

mandibles
The jaws or mouth-parts of insects.

medieval
Of the years known as the Middle Ages in Europe, from around AD1000–1500.

Medusa
One of the Gorgons (see above).

Minotaur
Greek monster, part man, part bull.

Mokele-Mbembe
A creature like a dinosaur, believed to live in swamps and forests in Central Africa.

mythical
From an ancient story (myth) often about gods and goddesses.

nomads
People who move from place to place.

Nordic
From Scandinavia (Norway, Denmark and Sweden).

nymph
A minor goddess from ancient Greece.

outcast
Someone rejected by their community.

ora
Another name for the Komodo dragon, a (real) large lizard that lives in Indonesia.

patron saint
Guardian saint of a country or a particular group of people.

Paracas
A civilization from Peru, in South America, powerful around 2000 years ago.

Phanesii
Monsters with enormous ears, from northern Europe.

plaque
Flat slab of clay or stone, decorated with pictures or writing.

roc (or rukh)
Enormous bird monster from the Middle East and the Indian Ocean.

sacrifices
Offers made to the gods to ask for their help or win their favour.

satire
Book or play that makes fun of the way people behave.

Saxon
A period of English history, from around AD500–800. The Saxons were farmers from Germany who settled in England.

Sciapods
Monsters with one huge foot, from Asia.

selkies
Seals who turn into beautiful women, reported in Scottish legends.

Shinto
The ancient religious faith of Japan, which honours spirits in the natural world and the spirits of dead ancestors.

shunned
Kept away from.

Simurgh
A magical bird-monster from the Middle East.

sinister
Evil.

Sirens
Beautiful sea-women from ancient Greece, who sang and lured sailors to their deaths.

Taotie
Monsters from ancient China. Dead ancestors that have been transformed into creatures with claws and horns.

totem
A spirit helper; often a dead ancestor.

totem pole
A tall wooden pole carved with totems, from North America.

triton
A sea-monster from ancient Greece with the body of a man but a tail like a huge fish.

trolls
Fierce, strong monsters from northern Europe. They live deep underground.

valiant
Bold and brave.

Villis
Ghostly spirits from eastern Europe who look like beautiful women, but who lure young men to their death.

were-jaguar
Part jaguar, part human Olmec god.

Yowie
A huge hairy monster, described in Aboriginal legends from Australia.

zombie
A monster with no mind of its own. A dead person brought to life by a magician.

INDEX